IT'S NOT JUST

STORIES & RECIPES FROM THE TIFF'S TREATS KITCHEN

TIFFANY CHEN AND LEON CHEN

FOUNDERS OF TIFF'S TREATS

HARPER HORIZON

To our parents, who have provided
unwavering love and support.
To Taylor and Tristan, who have brought
boundless joy into our lives.
And to Laine, who we dearly miss, for nudging
us in the right direction at the right time.

CONTENTS

INTRODUCTION

Tiff and Leon

Cookies were burning in the oven. Customers were on the phone, asking if their cookie delivery was on the way. The packaging table was backed up with cookies cooling off before we could get them boxed up warm.

"It's just cookies. Calm down," we'd often say to each other, as a way to stay focused. We'd rationalize that what we were doing wasn't a matter of life or death—therefore, we shouldn't let customer complaints and the stress of a fast-paced business ruin our day.

What started out as a two-person operation from our college apartment has grown to almost 100 locations with more than 2,000 employees, $100 million raised from investors, and a valuation in the hundreds of millions of dollars. However, Tiff's Treats only started because of a dating mishap in college. The story that follows, from that first moment to today, is unbelievable, even to us.

Over the years, both the business and the relationship should have failed multiple times. Our tale involves a gauntlet of misadventures more than a series of calculated moves. The journey included a crash course on how to run and scale a business, and along the way, we also learned many important life lessons.

Unexpectedly, we started an industry that didn't exist. The concept was simple: we'd bake to order cookies and deliver them while still warm from the oven. We had no idea we were "on-demand delivery" long before that was a thing. When we shared kitchen space with a restaurant in the early days, we didn't know that nearly twenty years later, "ghost kitchens" would also become a trend. We thought all we were doing was selling cookies. We didn't realize it was about so much more.

Many years later, we understood that we weren't just in the cookie business: we were in the business of connecting people through warm moments. We've witnessed some of the most amazing, inspiring moments and connections between people, while they were sharing or sending a batch of cookies. We've realized that we get a front-row seat to human nature at its best, with cookies as the conduit. And we're excited to share some of these stories with you.

Of course, no story of Tiff's Treats would be complete without talking about cookies. When we started the business, we focused on making the best version of the classics: chocolate chip, oatmeal raisin, peanut butter, and others. Over time, to pair with our classic cookie menu, we've added special, more adventurous weekly flavors. In this book, we've included recipes for homemade versions of some of our favorites. Keep in mind, we're not expert bakers. We were two kids who turned our hobby into a business, which happened to explode over the course of a couple decades. So we've learned a few things about baking along the way. The recipes are fun and easy, one thing that makes cookies such a crowd-pleaser as your go-to dessert. We hope you have as much fun baking these treats as we had creating them.

In our early days, we had many doubters. Someone close to us once posed a critical question: "What are you going to do, bake cookies for the rest of your life?" Ultimately, the answer was yes. Yes—but so much more. Building Tiff's Treats has been an adventure unlike any other, and as we've learned along the way, it's *not* just cookies.

CHAPTER I

A SWEET BEGINNING

Leon

We both grew up in Dallas and were friends in high school. There's some contention between us as to whether we went to our prom together as dates or friends. Tiff says we were just friends. Without going into detail, let's just say I got much more than the "friend" vibe. I mean, our first kiss was at prom.

In 1997 we started officially dating, during our freshman year at the University of Texas at Austin. We were both eighteen. Tiff was a creative advertising major; my major was marketing. We were living the normal lives of fairly serious college students—partying hard, studying a bit harder. Until the fateful December day when Tiff stood me up for a date and apologized by bringing me a batch of her warm chocolate chip cookies. It gave me a crazy idea. I came from an entrepreneurial family, and I was always figuring out businesses to start, whether selling baseball cards as a kid or buying and renting out margarita machines in college.

Hanging together in 1999, just as our business was starting

Tiff

To say that I stood him up on a date may be overstating the situation a bit, although it's technically true. We were already boyfriend and girlfriend, so this wasn't a first-date situation but more like plans we'd made to meet up and hang out. In any event, this was the '90s, so I was busy doing what you might expect: ice skating at the mall with my friends. I had no cell phone, and without a convenient way to call and say I was running late, I left him in the dark about when or if I would show up.

As a totally '90s sidenote, I did own a cell phone, a gift from my parents, which had to stay in the car at all times, in case of an emergency. And funny enough, the one time I did have an emergency it didn't work, and I had to walk to a payphone, since keeping the phone exclusively in my car meant it was never charged.

This wasn't an emergency, and I didn't walk to a payphone to call Leon. But when I returned home and explained the situation to my mom, she insisted I apologize. Baking cookies was something I'd been doing for years, and I was somewhat known for it during high school. I thought it would be the perfect olive branch.

I made my signature batch of from-scratch chocolate chip cookies and drove them over to his house. When I arrived, the cookies happened to be warm. He accepted my apology, and I headed home.

Leon

By the time Tiff got home from dropping off the apology cookies, I was on the phone, trying to convince her that we should start a warm-cookie delivery business, modeled on pizza delivery. I ran her through the plan: we would bake and deliver cookies to students, hot from the oven, make a ton of money, and have fun while doing it. I don't recall saying it was going to be "easy," but Tiff swears I also said that. She immediately said no to my idea, which wasn't surprising. I was always having ideas, and she was always telling me I was dreaming (still happens exactly this way all these years later). Freshman year, I told her I wanted to buy vending machines and put them all around campus, and she talked me out of that, making me feel stupid for even suggesting it. So after a few attempts at convincing her on the cookie delivery business, I gave up. I thought the idea was dead.

Then, an hour later, Tiff called from the grocery store to tell me she'd been pricing ingredients. I probably would have never brought up the idea of warm-cookie delivery to her again if she hadn't gone to the grocery store that day.

Tiff

I agreed to give Leon's idea a shot, with two conditions: I didn't want to quit or flunk out of college, and I wanted to have a social life and be a normal college student. We agreed that we'd go to class during the day and only do the cookie business part-time, Sunday through Thursday, 8:00 p.m. to midnight.

After settling on our hours, we had a few other basics we needed to nail down. We created a small menu of cookie flavors based on the ingredients I'd seen

Leon's apartment, which served
as our original location

available at the grocery store, and we researched how we would package the cookies. Using dial-up internet, we did some searching and stumbled upon a square white bakery box we thought could easily transport our warm cookies. Leon instantly had an idea. We could tie a ribbon around the box as a finishing touch. Our favorite café in our hometown tied their silverware packets with a colorful ribbon, and we always thought it was such a lovely addition. Little did we know that the white box with blue ribbon would eventually become our iconic

imagery, and that adding a simple detail to the box would lend perfectly to us becoming a gifting service on top of a snacking one.

Deciding on our "location" was easy; Leon had an apartment with a kitchen and we figured we could bake and deliver from there. But we needed a way for customers to place their orders. It was 1999. Cell phones were just becoming a thing, and we went to Austin's brand-new Sprint store and bought ourselves a flip phone. We wanted to sign up for a business listing, so people could look us up by name and/or see who was calling them on their caller ID. However, when they told us how expensive it was to get an account for a business listing, we decided to apply for our cell phone

An early marketing flyer

account using the name Tiffany S. Treats. On caller ID it would be easy to see the call was from "Tiffany's Treats."

Using our new phone number (Leon's personal cell number to this day), we printed a few hundred flyers and plastered them all over campus, including inside the dorms, which we used our UT IDs to sneak into. Then we returned to Leon's apartment, which he shared with two roommates, both friends of his since childhood, and waited for the phone to ring.

And waited.

For three days, the phone didn't ring.

Just when Leon was about to admit that warm-cookie delivery *was* a stupid idea, we got our first call. Cell reception and cell phones were so primitive back then. The message went right to voicemail. It took us a couple of hours to even realize someone had called.

A UT student named Amy had ordered a dozen cookies. Leon wrote down the details, then turned to me.

"Is Amy a friend of yours?" he asked.

I shook my head no.

"Well then," Leon said. "Maybe we do have a business after all."

BEG FORGIVENESS OR ASK PERMISSION?

Leon

As the orders started coming in, we forgot to pay attention to two tiny details.

One, we "forgot" it was illegal to operate a food-based business from a private home. That's what is special about being young, dumb, and naive—you don't know the rules, so you simply do what it takes to get your idea off the ground.

Two, we "forgot" to ask my two roommates' permission to turn their apartment into world headquarters of Tiffany's Treats, which included a bakery, distribution center, and administrative office.

The legal problem didn't bother us. Our whole operation was cross-our-fingers-and-hope-for-the-best. But we did feel bad about the roommates.

As time went on, my roommates, Stephen and Michael, had to put up with more and more disruption in their home, their oven (they had to scoot their frozen pizza rolls over to the side whenever we were baking), and their sleep. If it bothered my roommate Michael (I'm sure it did), he never complained. Years later, I asked him to be my best man at our wedding, and he'll always be one of my favorite people in the world. My other roommate, Stephen, was focused on studying for medical school. Wouldn't you know it? He also slept in the loft over the kitchen, which didn't have a door. We were regularly filling orders at midnight. Every time we took a sheet out of the oven, it woke him up. After "lights out" in the loft/living room, we'd wait in my bedroom for our phone to ring with orders. When a call came in, we'd tiptoe into the kitchen to put cookies on a baking sheet and in the oven.

One night, quite a few months in, Stephen and I had a big fight. Understandably, he wanted to know why we hadn't asked him before we started a business in the kitchen we all shared. I said to him, "You're good at school. You're going to go to med school. That's your opportunity. This is mine. This is my one shot at doing something I believe in. Tiffany's Treats is my med school, my one chance at success in life."

Even though he understood, it was a lot to ask. It took a while to mend our friendship, but today, Stephen is a successful radiologist in Austin, and he and I are good friends. Stephen even invited me to speak at a medical event he organized and is one of our biggest supporters.

THE CHOCOLATE CHIPS ARE IN THE SOCK DRAWER

Tiff

At seven o'clock every weeknight, an hour before we opened, we'd make a big batch of the basic dough we used for some of our flavors. When it was time to fill each order, we'd mix the other ingredients into as much dough as the order required.

There was zero room to store ingredients in the kitchen, so Leon cleared out the sock drawer of the dresser in his bedroom. The chocolate chips went on the left side of the drawer, and the M&M's went on the right. When someone placed an order for chocolate chip or M&M's cookies, we'd go into Leon's closet, reach into the ex-sock drawer, pull out the respective candies and mix them into our dough.

Most nights, the two of us would sit around watching a movie, playing a video game, or doing homework while we waited for the phone to ring. For the first few months, we averaged maybe three or four orders a night. Then five orders grew to about ten orders a night, which felt busy. After a particularly busy week, I remember Leon excitedly bragging to his friend Brian that we'd made over $300 in sales!

We'd targeted students as our market because *we* were students. After a while, we realized that students don't make the best niche market. They leave town for four months a year and when they order it's only a dozen at a time. Today, while we serve many colleges and universities, our focus is overwhelmingly on the corporate crowd. However, if we didn't start with college students, we probably wouldn't have made it in the beginning.

At one point we zeroed in on a sorority whose members regularly ordered. We realized that females made up a big portion of our customer base. They all interacted with each other, and word started spreading. We developed some solid customers at the Scottish Rite Dorm, and eventually word spread outside that demographic. This progression created enough critical mass to keep going. You have to start somewhere, with some group of people. For us, that group was college students.

OF COURSE WE CAN!

Leon

It wasn't just students who'd seen our flyers. The University of Texas administration had seen them too. And even though we'd snuck into places where we weren't allowed to post those flyers, and even though our little operation was driving my roommates nuts, and even though it was "illegal," the University of Texas called us—but not to expel or arrest us. They wanted Tiffany's Treats to cater the weekly summer orientation sessions for the parents of incoming freshmen. Their order: *seventy-five dozen cookies and fruit punch* to be delivered every Tuesday *at noon*.

The oven in my apartment could only fit two dozen cookies at a time. We did the math and calculated that it would take us twelve hours to bake seventy-five dozen cookies. (Today every Tiff's Treats location has the capacity to bake forty dozen cookies in fifteen minutes. But this is now. That was then.) We had two problems with this opportunity. First, our concept was warm-cookie delivery, and there was no way we could deliver seventy-five dozen cookies warm. Second, we had a rule that we wouldn't skip classes for the business. Baking that many cookies *and* delivering them at noon meant breaking that rule.

We were already struggling to balance our schoolwork with our blossoming business. Our college courses involved a lot of group projects that required meeting outside class time. Our classmates wanted to meet at night. Plenty of them had part-time jobs, but they could switch their shifts to do their schoolwork. But we were open Sunday to Thursday every week. We couldn't meet with those groups, which meant we couldn't do our academic work. It was tough watching our grades start to sink. But we had no choice if we were going to give Tiffany's Treats a chance.

At first, our classmates would be frustrated with us when we said we could never meet, but when we offered to deliver cookies to them during the meeting instead of being there ourselves, they soon forgave us.

Also, for the big UT order, we had no idea how to incorporate beverages into our business. We didn't even know how to make punch. We had to figure out how to do that, just like we'd figured out everything else we didn't know how to do, until we did it. We bought some big Igloo coolers and punch mix, and mixed up vats of punch. Then we seat-belted the

Baking cookies in our college apartment "location"

Igloo coolers into the back seat of Tiff's red Mustang and hauled them to the catering site. The punch would slosh around in Tiff's car as she was driving, spilling punch everywhere. We have never done punch since.

We charged UT next to nothing for these orders, because we didn't know how to price our products either. We had almost no expenses, so we charged a dirt-cheap price. UT got a great deal, and we got a great order. We gambled on them, and they gambled on us. It's crazy to think that one of the largest universities in the United States would order cookies from two students who didn't even have a real kitchen or storefront.

In this way, the best thing that had ever happened to Tiffany's Treats gave us our first lesson in compromise. We didn't have a choice. The UT order was all that stood between the beginning and the end of our business. So we started baking on Monday nights and kept baking on Tuesday mornings. We delivered cookies at various degrees of warmth at noon on Tuesdays.

Shortly after we started baking for the UT orientation sessions, we got a call from a parent who'd attended one of them. She worked in downtown Austin, and she wanted to know if we could deliver cookies to her office. We only had one answer to that question, the same answer we'd given UT when they asked us to deliver to their orientations: "Of course we can!"

Of course, we couldn't. The UT deliveries were already straining our ability to keep our grades up, and this commitment would push us over the line. Office workers don't want their

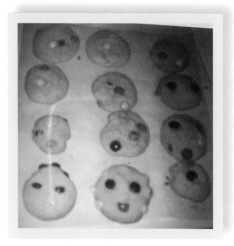

Tiff and Leon cookies, secretly added to our big order

warm cookies delivered between eight o'clock and midnight!

"Maybe for a big order, we could skip class," Tiff said to me. I was excited to get orders and hated class, so I readily agreed. We then discussed what constituted a big order. The majority of our customers were students who ordered for themselves and whomever they were hanging out with late at night, and their orders were small.

We decided that an order of four dozen was enough to justify missing class. That first big catering order from UT changed our whole trajectory. It broadened our reach from a small number of students to all the office workers in Austin. Even as our business expanded, we were determined to keep giving each order the personal touch: we'd sneak in a "Leon" cookie and a "Tiff" cookie, whenever we had time to make one of each. We used M&M's to create smiley faces, with blonde hair and blue eyes for her, brown hair and brown eyes for me.

Soon we were making daily deliveries to doctors' offices and law firms and downtown office buildings—and we attended class only as much as we needed to graduate. Luckily in those days, the professors didn't take attendance. If they had, we both would have flunked out. The year after we graduated, we heard that the university was starting an attendance policy.

During those college years, we were like the proverbial frog in a pot of water, with the heat gradually being turned up and up and up. When we started Tiffany's Treats, we vowed to work only sixteen hours a week and devote the rest of our time to school. By the end of our senior year, we'd increased to forty hours a week, and we were used to it, like the frog in boiling water. We didn't have the college life our friends had. We didn't have a lot of freedom. When our friends went on random trips, we couldn't go. We couldn't even take a night off and go to the movies.

But we have no regrets. In hindsight, meeting the demands of the University of Texas order was worth it. Those corporate orders are our bread and butter. It's amazing to think that we got our start because our own university was willing to take a chance on us and support one of its own. We'll forever be grateful to UT for giving us the chance and supporting us along the way.

THE BUSINESS PLAN IS: TRY TO STAY IN BUSINESS

Tiff

One reason for the early success of Tiffany's Treats was our overhead. To be specific, we had almost none. We were working out of Leon's apartment, so our only operational costs were ingredients, bakery boxes, gas for my red Mustang (aka our delivery vehicle), and the cell phone that served as our corporate phone system. Our low costs allowed us to price a dozen cookies at five bucks, which made our cookies an "affordable luxury" for our student market.

Elements of the business that we take for granted today were major breakthroughs back then. In the early days, our business consisted of delivering a dozen cookies at a time to a student in a dorm, for self-consumption. Then one day, someone called our cell phone and said he wanted to send cookies to his girlfriend. He asked if we could handle an order like that. "Of course!" we said.

Today, gifting cookies is a big portion of our business. Twenty years ago, though, we had absolutely no idea what gift orders would mean to our company or, for that matter, how to fulfill them. The fact that people order our cookies as much for themselves as they order to send as a gift is quite unique for any brand. People aren't sitting around an office asking one another if they want to go in on a "fruit bouquet" for an afternoon snack. They also aren't ordering pizza delivery for their business clients as thank-you gifts. However, with Tiff's Treats, it's socially acceptable to do both.

THE SPUDNIK PERIOD

Tiff

After about a year, our business was outgrowing the apartment. Even though we had bought a dedicated mini fridge to store the dough in the garage, we needed a change. Not only did we lack the space, but we were located too far from our core customers on campus and downtown, which made delivery times suffer. It was time for us to rent a commercial kitchen.

We searched all over town and quickly realized we couldn't afford our own kitchen. So we got creative, as we tend to do in seemingly impossible situations, and looked for any restaurant that might have spare space we could rent. We were met with resounding nos.

One day, our sales rep for *Ad Pages* magazine, a coupon booklet where we advertised,

Posing in front of our
first set of ovens

told us one of his other clients needed help—a baked-potato company called Spudnik. Carbs had been all the rage in the 1990s, but the fad was passing, and Spudnik wasn't doing well and could use some extra rent money. We raced up to the restaurant and excitedly asked the person at the counter for the owner, both speaking at the same time so quickly that she had to stop us and ask us to speak one at a time. "Do you have space to rent?!" is what then came out in unison. Turns out, she was the owner and yes, they were happy to share their kitchen with us for a small monthly fee. We moved in immediately and bought and installed a set of used residential ovens to call our own. Otherwise, the kitchen was totally shared. Us baking cookies on one table and their prep chef chopping onions on the next.

One interesting sidenote is that the space was attached to the Church of Scientology, which served as the landlord, and we shared a hallway and bathroom with them. We were fortunate to snag the kitchen-sharing arrangement, and the situation was the perfect way to bridge those next few years, upping our capacity, reducing delivery times, and as a bonus, adhering to local laws! We were now a licensed kitchen and even got our ingredients delivered by tacking onto the restaurant's orders from a legitimate food-supply company. Before then, I'd been shopping at Sam's Club weekly, hauling fifty-pound bags of flour and sugar into the trunk of my car. If you've ever wondered if it's easy for a five-foot-tall girl to load heavy, flopping bags of baking ingredients into a Mustang while also keeping the cart with the rest of her order from rolling off in the parking lot, I'm here to tell you it's not.

Another huge benefit was that we had a place where customers could come pick up their orders. Instead of delivery-only, you could place an order, and we'd bake it for you to come pick up at the restaurant. You had to come up to the counter at the potato restaurant and ask for us in the back, but still. It was kind of like having a real location. And the people in Austin were more than game to frequent our little speakeasy.

YOU CAN'T SEE AROUND THE CURVE, EVEN WHEN YOU'RE AHEAD OF IT

Leon

Looking back, we were ahead of the curve on a few things. We were doing on-demand food delivery twenty years before DoorDash and Postmates and Grubhub. We were sharing a commercial kitchen space with another small food business, long before doing that became as popular as it is today with "ghost kitchens." Later, we'd create our own software to computerize our operations, something else we were way ahead of other brands on.

Creating a formerly nonexistent industry has distinct advantages. It's easier to get market share when you're the only one offering what you're offering—in our case, warm-cookie delivery. Starting a business is hard enough; having zero competition makes it a lot easier. We also weren't limited by any preconceived notions of how something "should be," because there wasn't anything to compare ourselves to, which allowed us to just build the best business we could build.

Inventing a concept has plenty of downsides as well. One of the most challenging things was that, with the exception of cookie ingredients, we couldn't get anything off the shelf. Equipment, software—everything that existed to solve other people's problems didn't solve ours. We had to create a lot from scratch. In the early years, this was a downside because nothing came easy for us. However, this was also our biggest opportunity. For example, we couldn't find off-the-shelf software. Since a big component of our business was gifting, none of the pizza delivery software would work. So we were forced to build our own software, which became one of our biggest competitive advantages.

Since no one else was doing what we were doing, we had to educate our customers. No one knew how to be a customer of a warm-cookie delivery service. If you start a pizza place or a sub shop, people know how to buy a slice or a sandwich. We had to train our customers to place their orders by phone, first, and then online. They had to train us too! Some of our best ideas, like the idea of delivering to third parties instead of just to the person who placed the order—the gifting concept—came from customers' requests.

Another weird thing about creating a new business concept is that it can be hard to get people to take you seriously. We had a lot of doubters who basically said, "If this was such a great idea, someone would be doing it already." Eight years into running our business, friends and family members were still asking us what we *really* did for a living. They'd look at us as if they were questioning our sanity.

Sometimes we questioned that ourselves.

TIPS FOR BAKING A TIFF'S-STYLE COOKIE

Before we share our most famous recipe, Chocolate Chip Cookies, here's some advice that will help you make and enjoy the recipes throughout the book to their fullest extent.

- Let the butter soften all the way. You can set it out on the table for at least an hour or pop it in the microwave for a few seconds. You should be able to see your thumbprint in it, but it shouldn't be melted.
- If a recipe calls for chips, you can play around with how many you want, but measure everything else precisely, especially the flour. Measuring in a metal cup and using a knife to level off the flour is the easiest way to make sure it's accurate. Eyeballing the amount in a glass measuring cup meant for liquids can lead to incorrect proportions.
- Don't get carried away with the amount of dough in each scoop. If you make the doughballs too large, they won't hold their shape or bake through as consistently.
- Take the cookies out of the oven a bit before they look done. Slightly underbaked centers result in gooey cookies with lots of flavor. The cookies will set up and flatten as they cool down.
- Let the cookies cool a few minutes before eating, but whenever possible, serve warm! We've built a whole business around this philosophy, and it does make a difference.
- Store extras as soon as they are fully cooled, in something airtight like a ziplock bag, a tin, or Tupperware. They'll keep for several days. In the rare instance when they don't all get eaten, you can freeze extras for a longer shelf life. This has never happened to me, so I've never tried it. But I hear it works.

The cookie that started it all. Chocolate Chip Cookies are as classic as it gets, and of course, I made these cookies for my apology batch for Leon. Chocolate Chip Cookies outsell all of our other flavors combined. We make ours the traditional way, with semisweet chocolate chips. Semisweet chocolate is my favorite to use in cookies. It's sweet enough to be decadent without being overly heavy like dark chocolate, it's not as sugary sweet as milk chocolate, and it pairs perfectly with buttery, salty cookie dough.

This recipe is my homemade version of a Tiff's Treats Chocolate Chip Cookie—not precisely the same, but inspired by the company recipe and formatted for home baking. All the recipes in this book are inspired by a Tiff's Treats flavor, but each recipe has been tweaked for home baking and is intended to be reminiscent of, not identical to, a Tiff's cookie. I'm excited to share this Chocolate Chip Cookie recipe with you, so it can become your go-to staple.

CHOCOLATE CHIP COOKIES

PREP TIME: 10 MINUTES

BAKE TIME: 9 TO 11 MINUTES

MAKES 2 $^1/_2$ DOZEN COOKIES

- - - - - - - - - - - - - - - - - - -

1 $^1/_8$ cups (2 $^1/_4$ sticks) salted
    butter, softened
1 cup granulated white
    sugar
$^1/_2$ cup firmly packed light
    brown sugar
2 large eggs
2 teaspoons vanilla extract
1 $^1/_2$ teaspoons salt
$^1/_2$ teaspoon baking soda
2 $^1/_4$ cups all-purpose flour
1 (12-ounce) package
    semisweet chocolate
    chips

Preheat the oven to 375 degrees.

In a large mixing bowl, cream the butter, white sugar, and brown sugar together using a hand/electric mixer on medium speed until the mixture is smooth.

Add the eggs, vanilla, salt, and baking soda to the butter mixture. Mix on medium speed until the ingredients are incorporated and smooth.

Add the flour. Mix on low speed until the flour is no longer loose, then on medium speed until the flour is fully incorporated.

Add the semisweet chocolate chips and mix until incorporated fully.

Line a cookie sheet with parchment paper. Using a medium-sized cookie scooper, scoop cookie dough (approximately 2 table-spoons each) onto the cookie sheet, placing the scoops at least 2 inches apart.

Bake for 9 to 11 minutes, until the edges are browned and set.

Slide the parchment paper with cookies off the cookie sheet and directly onto the counter for cooling. (If not using parchment paper, let the cookies sit for 1 minute and then remove them to cool on the counter or a wire rack.)

Serve warm.

CHAPTER 2

JUST A COUPLE OF LOSERS

LOSING MONEY

Leon

As we approached college graduation and all of our friends were interviewing for jobs, Tiff and I had no idea what we should do. We were working on the business at night but weren't making anywhere near enough sales to support ourselves after graduation. However, we felt something special was going on. There was a buzz about what we were doing.

At the end of college, we were skipping school so often to deliver cookies to downtown businesses that we thought maybe there was an opportunity to expand. But that meant we'd have to risk it all and commit to doing this as our full-time job and career. Looking at our numbers, we didn't know how we could run the business and pay our bills. We'd been fortunate enough to have our parents financially support us while we were in college, but upon graduation, that would end. I remember telling a friend who asked what

UT graduation day!

Our short-lived late-night location on 6th Street

my post-college plans were going to be that I was thinking about getting a job at Dell while working on the business. I'm not sure why I said that. I must have thought that was the sensible thing to say, but I knew deep down I had to go all-in on the business for it to have a chance.

The next three years were a blur, as we worked hundred-hour work weeks, seven days a week. A typical work week would have us at the store no later than 9:00 a.m. and working until we closed at midnight. On weekends we opened later, so we could "sleep in," go in at 11:00 a.m., and work until midnight. For a while during those three years, we also had a walk-up location on 6th Street that was open until 2:00 a.m. on weekends, so one of us would work at that location, while the other went home after midnight to rest. We had a small but growing staff to help us, but we had to work those long hours to make payroll. After those midnight shifts, we were exhausted but also extremely hungry because a lot of times we were so busy we had to skip dinner. I remember driving home in silence at 12:30 a.m. and turning to Tiff to ask her if she was more hungry or more tired. Depending on the day, she might say "hungry," and that meant we'd forgo an extra hour of sleep to stop and grab something to eat on our way home. If she said "more tired," that meant we'd go straight home and get that precious extra hour of sleep. But that also meant no dinner.

Tiff

The first years post-graduation didn't happen the way I expected. I'd been involved in lots of activities while growing up, so I was used to getting up early, staying up late, and having a packed daily schedule. We'd invested a lot of hours into the business while we were in college, so plenty of hard work was going on then. But I wasn't quite ready for the morning-to-night requirements of our new life. I'd imagined that we'd hire staff and split the hours between us and them. Leon quickly set me straight that we had no money for that—we'd work every hour the business was open.

This way of life took some getting used to, and the first year was challenging. It didn't help that our store was near campus, so coming off a twelve-hour shift meant certain unpleasantries, like getting to your car and realizing someone had dumped an entire smoothie on it. Or having to bang on the window to make a drunk college guy stop peeing on your *glass* front door after closing.

During this time, we didn't pay ourselves except for the tips we earned on deliveries, which we took turns doing. I had a bit of leftover savings from my college fund, and Leon opened credit cards and charged all of his expenses. We lived modestly and were fortunate to be young with little personal overhead and no family to care for. We ate fast food every meal, frequenting 7-Eleven because their hot dogs were available before we needed to start our shift, and we were tired of breakfast foods. Even so, because of the stress and lack of sleep, we lost weight.

At the end of one of these first years, we had someone do our books. We'd lost $13,000. We used to joke about ways we could have spent $13,000 and had more fun—like driving down the road with the windows down and tossing out dollar bills as we went. Instead, we'd spent the money working the most grueling and stressful year we'd ever had, not paying ourselves, then *owing $13,000* at the end of it all. We had no business staying open. My checking account regularly had less than fifty dollars, and I had no savings.

Yet the situation was always improving. Sales were increasing, and while the growth was slow and not enough to pay the bills, it was enough for us to think quitting wasn't an option. People were excited about what we were doing. Why would we quit when things were on an upswing?

LOSING OUR SHARED KITCHEN

Leon

Working all the time for no pay was difficult enough, and many other challenges those first few years constantly made us question our own sanity for continuing with the business. At the end of college and the first half-year after college, we'd shared that kitchen space with the baked potato shop owners, Kate and Miguel. We became good friends with them, despite us being completely different from them. Tiff and I grew up in the suburbs and were preppy kids with a middle-class upbringing. Kate and Miguel were skaters and punk rockers, had grown up differently, and had little to no parental help or support.

Working in our shared kitchen

They'd wanted help paying the rent, so they let us share the space with them and were also nice enough to help us along the way. We used to go to the grocery store for all of our ingredients because our order volume wasn't big enough to have it delivered through a food-service company. Kate and Miguel let us tack onto their food-service order, so we could get ingredients delivered. They saw us taking phone orders by hand and helped us set up QuickBooks, which let us take orders electronically and save order history. They even helped us revise our website to bring it up to date.

To help them make rent, we loaned them $5,000 in cash, which we pulled from a line of credit from the bank.

A few months later, despite our help, they sat us down to tell us they were going out of business. We were terrified.

Of course, we were distressed that we weren't being repaid on money we had borrowed ourselves. Though the relationship ended on a sour note, looking back, we have nothing but gratitude for Kate and Miguel, who did the best they could and helped two younger entrepreneurs learn about business.

They moved their equipment out in the middle of the night. Before they did, they warned us that the landlord might seize our equipment to try to sell it off to recoup missed rent payments. We couldn't afford for that to happen, so Tiff and I hatched a plan. We rented a big moving truck, and the morning after Kate and Miguel moved out, we also moved out our equipment, stored it in the back of the truck, and parked the truck across the street.

Then I went next door to speak to the landlord. Once we introduced ourselves, we begged them to let us rent out the whole space, which cost $2,200 a month. At first they said no. The landlord told us they'd been under orders from Scientology Headquarters in LA to take over the whole building eventually.

We were heartbroken because we would have had to close the business when we were *just* starting to see momentum. If we could find a way to hang on, we could build a real business.

After much pleading, we struck a deal with the landlord. They'd let us rent the entire space on a month-to-month basis, with no guarantee as to when they'd need it back. But they'd give us a forty-five-day notice to vacate when that time came. We didn't know if we'd be allowed to stay one month or one year or longer, but we were thrilled that the business would survive at least another forty-five days. Not having the security of a long-term lease kept me awake many nights, stressing about our future if and when that forty-five-day notice arrived.

LOSING OUR SH*T

Tiff

Now that we had the restaurant space to ourselves, we set about making it our own. We turned a sliding window on the side of the building into a walk-up storefront where customers could buy individual cookies. Ultimately, it was faster to sell them ready-made cookies than to explain that they had to order first, then come back after we'd baked them. Our primary business was (and is) freshly baked *warm*-cookie delivery and preordered pick-ups hot from the oven. For some people, however, planning ahead isn't an option, and we needed to provide them with something immediate.

We ordered new signage and repainted the side of the building with our name, Tiffany's Treats, by hand using a stencil. I don't know how we got that to look halfway decent, considering that most of Leon's and my paint jobs at home have ended in disasters, requiring curtains to be hung on a wall with no windows, to cover the horrendous job we did edging where the wall and ceiling meet. Painting skills aside, we were excited to have our own place. Tiffany's Treats was on its way!

A walk-up location to call our own!

Then came the flood. In Texas we have thunderstorms, but that particular day we experienced a mild tornado. What we didn't know was that the pipes in the building weren't installed correctly, and when the water rose too high outside, the sewage system started working in reverse and overflowed out of the pipes and into our kitchen. Imagine a fountain of water gushing from every floor drain at full force. And when I say "water," I mean sewage. To contain the overflow, I even turned a large bucket upside down on a drain and sat on it, but the intensity pushed me off. We rushed to turn off the ovens before the water reached the outlets and called to let customers know their orders weren't coming.

"Like, at all?"

"Correct. We are knee-deep in water (and then some) and cannot get you your cookies."

Finally, the storm cleared, and we started mopping water and sewage out our front door. We even had a customer stop by to try to buy cookies as he watched us clean. I suppose we knew we had something special when people would brave a severe storm just to buy cookies, not minding that we were soaked and cleaning up a huge mess. The next few days were spent cleaning and sanitizing and tossing out everything that got wet and dirty.

Our hand-painted sign

LOSING MY MIND

Leon

Early on, every day felt like we were fighting to survive. Every day we had to overcome a new challenge, but we figured the hardships were all part of the typical startup story. We needed to stay focused on growing our business. Surprisingly, we seldom thought about quitting, even when we were tired, hungry, broke, and sad. However, I'll admit that after this sewage flood incident, I wondered if maybe we weren't destined to have a successful business. We could discount normal hardship as everyday challenges, but as I cleaned up after the flood, I wondered if it was a sign we were in the wrong line of work.

The sewage explosion and more happened right around the same time. We experienced one setback after another on an almost weekly basis. It felt like we were constantly treading water. To say it was a stressful period would be a major understatement. Tiff and I deal with stress in completely different ways. When she gets stressed, she's good at compartmentalizing that stress. For me, being worried about something consumes me, and it's hard for me to focus on anything else.

Because of the stress, for the first time in my life, my health became an issue. Up until that time, I'd always been extremely healthy. I played sports and ate well and never had any physical issues. As we worked those hundred-hour work weeks, all we ate was junk food, and we didn't have time for fitness.

The problems started on a random day, when I felt shooting pains in my head. It was so bad I thought I was having a stroke. Then, at random times I'd start feeling faint, and I'd struggle to breathe. It got so bad that one day at the store, I was having trouble holding a tray of cookies and putting it in the oven. I didn't know what was going on. Maybe it was a stroke; maybe it was a heart issue. It was terrifying. I immediately went to the emergency room, thinking something bad was happening.

At the ER the doctor asked me questions, ran a whole bunch of tests, and sent me home wearing a heart monitor. We were beyond broke, so I was asking how much everything would cost. The ER doctor made me feel foolish by shrugging at my questions about cost and saying, "I don't know. You have insurance—why does it matter?" What she didn't realize was that I didn't have insurance. I was out thousands of dollars that I didn't have for ER and medical bills, thus adding to the stress. After my heart monitor results came back all clear, I was sent for an MRI on my brain, which also came back all clear. Some days were better than others, but then I felt the shooting pains in my head again and went back to the ER.

During this second ER visit, I was describing my previous visit and everything I'd gone through, and the doctor confidently told me, "You're having panic attacks." I didn't want to believe it. However, the doctor was sure and prescribed me medication that turned me into a bit of a zombie (but did make me feel better).

In the weeks and months that followed, I had to wean myself off the medication and learn to manage my stress. Whenever I felt a panic attack coming on, I learned to calm myself down, and eventually the attacks subsided. I haven't had a panic attack in over a decade, though there have been various work and life stresses (for instance, having twins did not help my stress levels). It was a learning experience for me at a young age, and even though it was scary and cost money I didn't have, I'm grateful I went through it. The experience taught me I had to prioritize mental and physical health. I realized that if I planned to continue with the ups and downs of building a business, I'd have to be in the best possible shape. Managing stress and focusing on all aspects of health is something I have to work on every day.

LOSING OUR NAME

Tiff

One day, Leon returned from checking our mail. "Can you give me all the names of the downtown law firms who order from us?" he asked. This didn't sound good. When we'd filed a trademark on our name, we'd gotten on Tiffany & Co.'s radar. They wanted us to stop using the name Tiffany, or any form of it. The smart thing to do would have been to rebrand, but we were in our early twenties, so the three years we'd spent with the name Tiffany's Treats seemed like a lifetime. We didn't think it was possible to change the name without losing our brand recognition. So Leon set out to interview various law firms about our defense, while I worked the store.

Leon

Tiffany & Co. was claiming trademark dilution, which meant their brand was so famous that even though we weren't in the same business, any use of their name would damage their brand. Every law firm wanted to fight this case for us because the law stated that in order for Tiffany & Co. to prove dilution, they had to prove monetary damages were associated, which would be nearly impossible. It was a dilemma for sure. We could fight for what we believed was our legal right or move on and give up the name. We settled on an attorney, Alicia Groos, at one of the firms downtown, who wasn't out to make a big name by taking the case to court. To us, it seemed that she was the only attorney who thought of how a lawsuit would affect us as business owners, psychologically and emotionally. Twenty years later, she's still our trademark attorney.

Tiff

Even trying to find a way to settle with Tiffany & Co. was extremely stressful because it would cost money and time we didn't have. But Alicia fought to allow us to shorten the name to Tiff's Treats. This came at a considerable cost, and while Leon was on a call with our attorneys, I'd regularly hold up countdown signs for him, stating the amount of time spent on the call so far and its coordinating dollar amount spent. In the end, we came to an agreement with Tiffany & Co. that we could use the name Tiff's Treats, after spending about $20,000 of borrowed money.

Ultimately, the shorter name was easier to say, and we liked it more. One unexpected result was that the cease-and-desist letter ultimately changed *my* name. Before, I was known to most people as Tiffany, and only a handful of friends called me Tiff. I introduce myself as Tiffany, but almost nobody calls me that anymore.

LOSING OUR LOCATION

Tiff

Just as we were filing away our legal issues and printing up our new name on our window (this time a fancy decal from Fastsigns instead of hand painting), we were hit with what had been hanging over our heads for a while: the forty-five-day notice to vacate the property. The Scientologists were reclaiming their entire building, and they needed us out.

Since we'd anticipated this at some point, we'd been working with a real estate broker who'd been showing us other properties. This is how we knew that no other spaces in the area were suitable for us, and even if one was, nobody was interested in renting to us in our current financial state. After hitting too many dead ends, we'd cut the broker loose.

This was time to panic.

Even if we'd had options, forty-five days isn't enough time to find a retail space, negotiate a lease, secure a permit, convert the space into a commercial kitchen, and open for business. On average, it currently takes us about a year to go from site selection to grand opening, and we work fast. But the good news is that we had no idea that it couldn't be done.

We drove around town, looking for out-of-the-box solutions to our problem. Eventually, between campus and downtown, we stumbled upon a small 1940s converted house, which was being used as a property management office, with a sign in the yard advertising a sublease! This was our chance. But we knew we couldn't make this happen on our own.

Leon

We needed someone to help represent us, and we met the first of our mentors, Mike Joyce, through the landlord of our failed 6th Street walk-up location. Mike was a local real estate broker who had an extensive background buying, operating, and selling over twenty small businesses. He contacted the landlord of the property management office, Dr. Schneider, who was in his late seventies. Dr. Schneider and his wife, Ellie, were successful and beloved in the Austin community and owned a decent amount of property around town. When Mike first approached Dr. Schneider about the possibility of leasing to us, we were immediately turned down. We were just two kids with no credit history and no history of profitability for our business. We later learned that many years before, at that exact property, Dr. Schneider had taken a chance on two young kids who owned a photography business—a bad experience that led to the place almost burning down! Understandably, he hesitated to take an unnecessary risk again.

Our first stand-alone storefront, a remodeled 1940s bungalow

However, Mike persisted and convinced Dr. and Mrs. Schneider to meet us. When we did, we immediately connected. They let us lease the space and trusted us to remodel this 1940s house into a commercial kitchen. With help from Tiff's mom, who put $10,000 in a CD as collateral for the lease, we finally had something we'd never had: a long-term lease. We didn't have any money to build the space, but we focused on one challenge at a time. Dr. and Mrs. Schneider gave us a chance when nobody else would. We were two broke kids, with a business losing money, wanting to lease their property. They had every reason to say no, but they were kind people who believed in us.

They became much more than our first landlords. They became our friends and even filled a sort of grandparent-type role in my life. Eight years later, they were guests at our wedding, and almost twenty years later (they're in their mid-nineties!), we stay in touch regularly. They both hold a special place in our hearts because Tiff's Treats likely wouldn't exist if they hadn't taken a chance on us.

Tiff

With the lease secured, we needed to move on to phase two: renovating a house into a commercial kitchen, something we'd never done. The first step was to create drawings to submit for a building permit. Architects and engineers typically do this, and it costs about $20,000. Obviously, that wasn't going to happen. Instead, I measured all of our equipment, roughly scaled it down, created tiny shapes using the dimensions, and printed it on a piece of paper. I then cut out the shapes and pasted them onto another paper, which had the house layout printed on it, and labeled everything. A quick trip to Kinkos to xerox it and voilà!—we had drawings.

Leon

We had about thirty days remaining before the Scientologists needed us out. If it took longer than that to build and permit, we wouldn't be able to sustain the business. So early one morning, I took Tiff's handmade building plan to the City of Austin Permitting and Development Center, signed in, and waited anxiously for them to speak with me. I knew how much was at stake and that it usually took a long time and many revisions to get a permit to remodel commercial space.

I was called back to meet the first inspector, and when he asked to see my plans, I

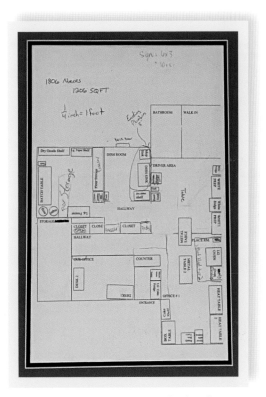

Official drawings we submitted for our first real location

pulled out Tiff's elementary-school-looking project on one piece of paper. The look on his face was a mix of confusion, pity, and curiosity. He kind of shook his head, and it looked like he was about to tell me to get out of his office. But I think he saw the desperation in my eyes. He asked what was going on, and I told him the entire story. I don't know if he felt sorry for me or if he thought what we were trying to pull off was impossible—therefore making what he was about to do next harmless—but he took me to every building department to get stamps of approval.

We walked through plumbing, electrical, and mechanical, and one by one, they each stamped their approval for the plan. I walked out of that office with permit in hand, having gotten the entire building permit in *one day*. Today, it would take us months and months to secure a permit to build a new store in Austin, with a lot of back and forth. But on that day, at that moment, a group of individuals in that office decided to help us in a way that still astonishes me.

Tiff

Now we needed to build the space. We found a contractor who agreed to do the remodel. In our initial meeting he asked me, "Do you want to do this the cheap way or the expensive way?"—which I find an odd question to ask a client. "Yes, the cheap way sounds perfect," I said. But even the cheap way came with a hefty bill.

By a stroke of luck, a few weeks before our forty-five-days-to-vacate notice had arrived, Leon and I had signed for a $100,000 line of credit at a nearby bank. For reasons I can't understand, they were loaning money to anyone (even us) with nothing more than a signature backing it up. I recall having asked Leon, "What is this for?" He replied that it was always a good idea to have cash available, just in case. If it weren't for that line of credit, we would have had no way to pay for the renovation. For all the hardships during this time period, we were equally bestowed with serendipitous good fortune.

"We have moved" signage posted on our original location

In a matter of weeks, we had the construction nearly finished and were planning our move, timing it so we were only closed one day. We couldn't afford to lose even one day of sales, but that was the best we could do. One day, we were met by the building inspector, who'd stopped by to tell us that after further review of our building plans, we'd need to install a vent hood over our oven in the new space. We both dropped to our knees on the sidewalk and begged: "We don't, we don't—I promise we don't." (I'm not sure if this is how it went down or if this is how I imagine it in my memory.) A vent hood would have cost $10,000 we didn't have and delayed our construction schedule, forcing us to close the store for weeks. Yet again, the stars aligned, and the inspector took pity on us. We talked her into allowing us to open without the vent hood, as long as we promised to install one later.

On an October day in 2003, we rented a truck and gathered all of our employees to help us move our equipment to our new location. We said a fond farewell to the ex-potato shop turned cookie store inside of a Scientology building. We were moving on to bigger and better things, but the time we spent in that place was filled with some of our most precious memories.

Moving a few blocks down the street into a stand-alone building was more than a survival move. It also proved strategic. We were now closer to the offices downtown, while within walking distance of campus. This helped position us for the corporate clientele we were beginning to attract. And the location had more visibility and better parking, both critical for our growing delivery business.

Being forced to move turned out to be the best thing for us. Within a few years, things started to turn in our favor, and we started seeing rapid sales growth. And that house serves as our flagship location and is one of our highest-producing stores.

It had been a rocky start, but now that we were settled, we were ready to start winning.

OREO cookies are just plain yummy, with that chocolate crunch and creamy center. These chocolate-based cookies are made softer and creamier with the addition of cream cheese. The idea came about when my daughter was four, and we were playing around with how we could incorporate OREO cookies into our Tiff's cookies. The original plan used the standard Chocolate Chip dough, but our dough production manager swapped in a chocolate-based dough, and this cookie was born!

COOKIES & CREAM COOKIES

PREP TIME: 10 MINUTES

BAKE TIME: 9 TO 11 MINUTES

MAKES 2 1/2 DOZEN COOKIES

7 (regular-size) chocolate
    sandwich cookies

5 (1.55-ounce) cookies and
    cream candy bars

1 cup (2 sticks) salted
    butter, softened

2 ounces cream cheese

1 cup granulated white
    sugar

1/2 cup firmly packed light
    brown sugar

2 large eggs

2 teaspoons vanilla extract

1 1/2 teaspoons salt

1/2 teaspoon baking soda

2 cups all-purpose flour

1/4 cup HERSHEY'S Special
    Dark Dutch Cocoa

1/2 tablespoon 2% milk

Preheat the oven to 375 degrees.

Place the chocolate sandwich cookies in a resealable storage bag, crush, and set aside.

Break the cookies and cream candy bars by hand into small to medium pieces and set aside.

In a large mixing bowl, cream the butter, cream cheese, white sugar, and brown sugar together using a hand/electric mixer on medium speed until the mixture is smooth.

Add the eggs, vanilla, salt, and baking soda to the butter mixture. Mix on medium speed until the ingredients are incorporated and smooth.

Add the flour and cocoa. Mix on low speed until the flour is no longer loose, then on medium speed until the flour is fully incorporated.

Add the milk and mix on low speed for a few seconds. Add the crushed cookies and cookies and cream candy bits, and mix on low speed until the ingredients are fully combined.

Line a cookie sheet with parchment paper. Using a medium-sized cookie scooper, scoop the cookie dough (approximately 2 table-spoons each) onto the cookie sheet, placing the scoops at least 2 inches apart.

Bake for 9 to 11 minutes, until the edges are browned and set.

Slide the parchment paper with cookies off the cookie sheet and directly onto the counter for cooling. (If not using parchment paper, let the cookies sit for 1 minute and then remove them to cool on the counter or a wire rack.)

Serve warm.

Note: Using standard unsweetened cocoa instead of HERSHEY'S Special Dark Dutch Cocoa will result in a lighter-colored dough with a less-rich chocolate flavor.

Though I'm a semisweet chocolate girl, our Milk Chocolate Toffee Cookie is my favorite limited-time flavor. I'm a sucker for toffee in almost any form, so when we add it to our cookies, that's instantly one of my preferred flavors—regardless of what kind of chocolate is in there with it. Toffee isn't a dream to work with; it sticks to the parchment paper and our spatulas when we're packaging the cookies in our stores. But the outcome is worth it, and I try to get this one on the menu as often as I can.

MILK CHOCOLATE TOFFEE COOKIES

PREP TIME: 10 MINUTES

BAKE TIME: 9 TO 11 MINUTES

MAKES 2 1/2 DOZEN COOKIES

- 1 cup (2 sticks) salted butter, softened
- 1 cup granulated white sugar
- 1/2 cup firmly packed light brown sugar
- 2 large eggs
- 2 teaspoons vanilla extract
- 1 1/2 teaspoons salt
- 1/2 teaspoon baking soda
- 2 1/3 cups all-purpose flour
- 1 (11.5-ounce) package milk chocolate chips
- 1 (8-ounce) package English toffee bits

Preheat the oven to 375 degrees.

In a large mixing bowl, cream the butter, white sugar, and brown sugar together using a hand/electric mixer on medium speed until the mixture is smooth.

Add the eggs, vanilla, salt, and baking soda to the butter mixture. Mix on medium speed until the ingredients are incorporated and smooth.

Add the flour. Mix on low speed until the flour is no longer loose, then on medium speed until the flour is fully incorporated.

Add the milk chocolate chips and English toffee bits, and mix on low speed until the ingredients are incorporated fully.

Line a cookie sheet with parchment paper. Using a medium-sized cookie scooper, scoop the cookie dough (approximately 2 tablespoons each) onto the cookie sheet, placing the scoops at least 2 inches apart.

Bake for 9 to 11 minutes, until the edges are browned and set.

Slide the parchment paper with cookies off the cookie sheet and directly onto the counter for cooling. (If not using parchment paper, let the cookies sit for 1 minute and then remove them to cool on the counter or a wire rack.)

Serve warm.

CHAPTER 3
EXPANDING OUR FOOTPRINT

Tiff

The minute we got comfortable and barely had our legs under us, Leon dropped a bomb-shell: "We need to open another location."

It was true that our warm-cookie delivery service was starting to take off, so much so that we'd rented a secondary kitchen space in downtown Austin to fulfill overflow deliveries. Were we ready to run multiple locations? Absolutely not. But we'd been in business for several years, and it was time.

We decided that our second location shouldn't be in another area of town but in a whole different city. Our Austin location serviced the downtown offices, and in our minds we (incorrectly) believed that our concept would only work in a densely populated downtown area, with many people working closely together in offices in a small delivery zone. Which meant that downtown Dallas (a 3.5-hour drive from Austin) would be the perfect next spot. Dallas was at least three times larger, which meant only one thing: we'd be three times busier! With this confidence, we set out to open our next location.

A real estate agent in Dallas showed us properties, and we settled on one in the heart of downtown but around the corner from the main street. We figured that since we did so much off-site business, the location didn't matter aside from its proximity to nearby offices. It wasn't until nearly five years later, after we opened our first highway-visible location in Houston, that we learned the importance of a location with lots of drive-by or walk-by traffic, to get eyeballs on your store.

Our first Dallas location

Ribbon cutting for our
first Dallas location

The Dallas store opened and had an abysmal amount of sales. It didn't help that in a shopping center that could fit ten retailers, only three of us were open. It was a ghost town, but that wasn't our only issue. We had one location that could service maybe a five-mile radius in a gigantic city. And it was a major struggle to gain name recognition with a nonexistent marketing budget. It made no sense to pay for advertising that would reach an entire city when you could only service a tiny portion (this was before the days of social media). Even downtown customers couldn't send gifts to their other clients in the Dallas area because we only had the one location, and we couldn't deliver very far.

We kept at it, but every day I worried that the magic we had in Austin wasn't going to work anywhere else.

Looking back, the sensible decision would have been to expand in Austin, where we easily could have overseen and managed all locations at the same time. We would've had built-in brand recognition and loyalty, and our mistakes would have been less costly. There was plenty more business to capture in our hometown, but we were too shortsighted to recognize that.

On the plus side, we received on-the-job training on how to manage a location remotely. We had transferred some of our best managers from Austin to the Dallas location, and our first stab at management was to let them feel ownership of their store. While we were extremely involved in running all business functions for the Dallas location, like marketing and accounting, we became so hands-off in the day-to-day running that they began to operate differently. During one visit, we found that they'd increased the doughball size, which in turn caused a need to increase the heat in the oven, which in turn created larger and crunchier cookies than those we were selling in Austin. Our big mistake was to assume that empowerment meant leaving them to their own devices, absent any procedures or support to make sure we were all running the same business. The solution was simple: we needed to meet face-to-face once a month. In those meetings we created processes and made decisions about how we'd update and improve operations, together.

We continued those meetings, and over the years, they eventually became Leadership Team meetings. Still held once a month, they serve as a gathering place for a cross-functional team composed of a trusted group, where we solve problems and make sure everyone is on the same page with all new initiatives before they're rolled out.

Even with lessons learned, the Dallas location continued to struggle. Thankfully, our Austin store was performing so well that its profits could roughly offset the losses in Dallas. However, it was painful to think that we'd finally found some success, only to squander it on a faltering location. But much like we'd seen in the early years in Austin, our Dallas customers were fanatical and loyal. Sales were increasing, albeit slowly, and we knew in our guts that it wasn't time to quit.

Leon

For a while, it was the worst of both worlds. Our downtown Dallas location was struggling, and I was so stressed out that I couldn't sleep. My stomach would knot as I worried about failing and going bankrupt. Tiff, amazing sleeper that she is, would snooze through most of my middle-of-the-night panics. One night, I looked at her while she was sleeping and resented her ability to compartmentalize. I shook her until she woke up.

"What do you want?" she asked.

"I can't sleep. We are so close to failing in Dallas. If we do, I don't know how the company is going to survive," I said.

Tiff always said the same thing: "Do we *have* to talk about this now? Can we talk about this tomorrow, please?" Two seconds later, she'd fall back asleep, while I'd toss and turn the rest of the night.

While the Dallas location was faltering, our Austin location was going bonkers with more daily orders than we could handle, which created a different kind of stress. We quickly opened a second Austin location in 2008, followed by a third location in 2009 to relieve pressure from the flagship Austin store. Those stores were an immediate hit, which gave us the first glimpse of how big the possibilities could be for the brand. In 2010 we returned to Dallas to open several more locations and found that with brand awareness under our belt, there was promise in that market after all.

A few years later, we decided to open in Houston. Early in the morning on grand opening day, as we drove up to help the team prep, we noticed quite a few people waiting in line wearing

Texas Longhorn shirts. As the day continued and the line grew, we noticed about 50 percent of the crowd in burnt orange and white, the school colors for the University of Texas. Entering a new market and seeing this kind of support made us emotional. It was as if Longhorn Nation was helping us will our way to success through their love and support. They were proud to show us our school colors.

Tiff

Our next market to tackle was San Antonio, a short drive from Austin. The timing of our first location there meant we'd have four-week-old babies when the store opened. I'd been involved in the building of the location before maternity leave and therefore had to field last-minute

The twins go on their first work trip!

calls from contractors and vendors while I was at home with newborns on the bed with me.

When it was time for the grand opening, there was no way I was going to miss it. I had been at every opening we'd had, and sitting at home wasn't an option. Leon and I packed up the babies, along with my mom and a car full of supplies. You'd have thought we were moving across the country instead of making an overnight trip an hour away. This was our first hotel stay with the babies. We reserved a separate room for Leon, since he'd be working on his feet the whole next day. My mom and I stayed up all night with the babies in our room. In the morning, I was exhausted but dead set on getting to the opening.

Our grand openings usually kicked off at 9:00 a.m., with a long line and fanfare of gift card giveaways and other celebrations. I wanted to be there when everything started. Yet as much as I tried, I couldn't get the babies fed and changed and dressed in time. On the way over, the clock hit 9:00 a.m., and I lost it. I was so overwhelmed, and the one thing that was important to me I couldn't even get done. It felt like everyone and everything in my world was passing me by.

But once I got there, I realized that my timing wasn't important. We were opening a new store; we had a flurry of excited customers, and I got to bring my babies to their first Tiff's Treats event. It was a nice, smooth day, and I'll always remember that the babies' first trip was for work.

Going on maternity leave meant I had to pass off all of the rote tasks I managed. When I returned to work, that was the perfect opportunity to pass those off permanently. It was a good pushing-out-of-the-nest moment, to move toward building teams that could do the work we'd been shouldering, allowing us to grow faster. And grow we did.

Leon

After opening in the four major Texas markets of Austin, Dallas, Houston, and San Antonio, we decided to take the brand to our first market outside of Texas. Our team did a ton of research on prospective markets and had a lot of productive internal debates about the matter. We wanted to minimize the variables we couldn't control for the first expansion out of our home state. At some point, we knew we'd have to learn how to deliver in ice and snow and in big cities with bikes and scooters. But we didn't want to have to learn all of that for our first non-Texas market. We also wanted a place that was similar to Texas as far as laws and regulations, and one with a vibrant business center and thriving culture.

We settled on Atlanta, Georgia, for our expansion. Unlike when we first expanded in Dallas, we already knew Atlanta would be a challenge. By then we knew what we had to do to build a brand and didn't want to take any shortcuts. We knew we could go in and sell cookies for a quick dollar, but our goal was to build our brand and immerse ourselves in the community. It was more important to us that we execute and build the brand loyalty carefully and thoughtfully, no matter the cost.

We arrived at 4:00 a.m. the morning of our first non-Texas grand opening, in Alpharetta, Georgia. People were already lined up, waiting for the 9:00 a.m. opening. When we walked up to the store, we recognized the first two people in line. Superfans Danny and Cynthia, whom we'd met at previous Texas openings, were so excited about our expansion that they drove overnight, for fifteen hours straight from Texas to Georgia, to be the first people in line for our first location outside of Texas.

Grand Opening event in Alpharetta, Georgia

The line for that store's opening was one of the longest we've ever had, wrapping around the building all day. At the end of the seven-hour event, we'd sold 1,500 boxes of one dozen cookies, with all sales that day going to a local charity. We were so excited about and touched by the outpouring of support that day. Some of them were Texas transplants who'd moved to Georgia, but most of them were people whose friends and families had spoken so highly of our brand that they wanted to come and experience it for themselves.

Tiff

Over the next year or so, we opened seven locations in the Atlanta area. True to our expectations, the going was tough. While we had a good-sized fan base awaiting our arrival, we needed more customers. We were a small brand with a small footprint, trying to spread the word in an enormous city. Even with seven locations, we struggled to make an imprint in such a massive market. But we'd seen this in most of our new markets and knew there was only one thing to do: be patient and diligently work to ingratiate ourselves to the community. Building our brand there would take time.

On the heels of the Atlanta expansion, we prepped to open our first location in Nashville. With a smaller market and similar in feel and culture to Austin, we were excited to approach something more manageable. After signing a lease and beginning construction, we began to give some serious thought to an endeavor we'd never before broached.

Nashville happened to be home to a company called Jake's Bakes, which had one location and operated with a similar business model as ours. Jake had attended the University of Texas at Austin years ago and created his own brand many years later, after moving to Nashville. This was the first time we'd encountered a competitor with not only our same operating model but also our same target clientele. Our board encouraged us to call Jake and offer an acquisition. Although we were already underway with building our own location, acquiring this company meant we'd have an instant customer base when we opened.

Jake turned down our first offer. We'd thought a good approach was to offer him a job on the Tiff's Treats team, in addition to the financial deal. That way, he'd be bought in and help us more seamlessly make the transition. From our initial conversations, we got the impression that he might be interested in a peripheral role, maybe something to do with marketing. Yet marketing was the one thing he hated doing. After sorting this out, we convinced him to spend a few days with us in Austin, so we could see if we could work out some arrangement.

When we met, talking to him was like traveling back in time. Every pain point he was experiencing was exactly what we'd gone through when our company was that same size. We hit it off, finding him to be cheerful, charismatic, bright, and capable. We knew right away that he was a fit for Tiff's Treats in a bigger way, and when we discovered that his real strength and passion was operations and people management, we were more than happy to offer him this role instead. Effective operators are hard to come by, and his particular skill set, being able to motivate a team, is difficult to teach.

When it came to enacting the acquisition, we had no idea what we were doing. Luckily, we had Lee Valkenaar on our board. He'd been through many mergers and acquisitions as an executive VP of Global Support at Whole Foods, and we met with him numerous times. He coached us through the more human side of the process—what the Jake's Bakes team might feel, how their customers might react. While I was busy figuring out the logistics of when to do the rebranding of their location and how to make the public announcement, he was warning us to be sensitive in our approach.

The next step was to head to Nashville and prepare Jake's team for the change. Their location would be remodeled and rebranded as a Tiff's Treats. Their customer list would be emailed about the change, and the website and all social media channels would be redirected to Tiff's Treats after the switch went live.

We met with every member of his team to introduce ourselves, and our director of human resources interviewed interested members for jobs at Tiff's Treats. We extended an offer to every one of them. As I said, Jake was great at people management, and he'd amassed a good and loyal team over the years. Most of them accepted the job, but a few declined. Several years later, some of them are still on the Tiff's Treats team, many having grown into leadership roles.

Winning over the customers was another story. On one hand, the acquisition strategy worked. An overwhelming amount of the Jake's Bakes customers were willing to try Tiff's Treats and loved it. Sales were bigger than we expected. But as Lee had warned us, a vocal minority despised us for shutting down their local institution. We were flooded with one-star reviews and negative comments about the taste of our cookies versus Jake's. They wanted Jake's Bakes

With Jake at the old Jake's Bakes location

back, and they weren't afraid to say it. I truly think they believed that enough harassment meant we'd switch back to being a Jake's Bakes. I also think they assumed we were a large company that had bullied a smaller one out of business, when we weren't all that big, and Jake himself was now a member of our team in a high position.

It was quite funny and awkward at times to drudge through dealing with these angry customers together with Jake. Some comments were even made to his face when he was working in the new Tiff's Treats store, with the customers unaware that he was Jake. I can't help but think that some of these mean comments brought a smile to his face. He's a nice guy, so he'll never admit it, but I'm sure it was satisfying to see how much his fans were missing his cookies. Over time, the comparisons dwindled, and we began to win over most of his customers and gain our own as well.

One thing you wouldn't necessarily think would be required for opening a warm-cookie delivery company: thick skin. We learned years ago to get used to all kinds of uncensored comments coming our way, both positive and negative, and because of that, we could find humor in all this.

We continued to expand in Nashville, with Jake at the helm. Jake remains a valuable member of the Tiff's Treats team, as director of operations for the Southeast region, and has been key in helping us grow and manage that region.

Leon

After Nashville, we continued with our expansion in the Southeast, opening in Charlotte, North Carolina, next. During this time, we continued to open more stores in our home state of Texas. We added stores in the big cities while also succeeding in smaller towns like Lubbock, Waco, and College Station. Our expansion is ongoing and we now open in new cities regularly.

Many brands equate the number of locations to success. Tiff and I have never felt that the number of stores should be the measure of success. We could easily triple the number of current stores, but from the beginning we decided to focus on quality over quantity. As we approach one hundred locations overall, we look to continue expanding throughout the United States, but only at a pace that allows us to responsibly grow without jeopardizing the quality of the brand.

Our expansion hasn't always been smooth—it's often been fraught with worry and doubt. We've learned and continue to learn lessons along the way.

And that original Dallas location? It became our best store in the entire system, outperforming even our flagship Austin location. It pumps out a volume of cookies that anyone would be shocked to witness: well over two million cookies each year. It just took some time.

When we first decided to try this flavor, we saw the finished product and I said, "There is no way we can sell these. They're blue!" But then I tasted one and realized there was no way we could *not* sell them. These scrumptious cookies taste exactly like blueberry muffins but with the sweet density of a cookie. Topped with sugar to create a crunchy shell, these sticky, soft treats are a surprising crowd-pleaser.

BLUEBERRY MUFFIN COOKIES

PREP TIME: 10 MINUTES

BAKE TIME: 12 TO 15 MINUTES

MAKES 2 ½ DOZEN COOKIES

1 cup (2 sticks) salted
    butter, softened
1 cup granulated white
    sugar
½ cup firmly packed light
    brown sugar
1 ½ cup fresh blueberries
2 large eggs
2 teaspoons vanilla extract
1 ½ teaspoons salt
½ teaspoon baking soda
2 ½ cups all-purpose flour
½ cup sanding sugar,
    optional

Preheat the oven to 375 degrees.

In a large mixing bowl, cream the butter, white sugar, and brown sugar together using a hand/electric mixer on medium speed until the mixture is smooth.

Lightly hand-mash the blueberries and add them to the butter mixture. Mix on medium speed until the blueberries are fully blended and the dough becomes pale blue in color. Some blueberry pieces will be intact.

Add the eggs, vanilla, salt, and baking soda to the mixture. Mix on medium speed only until the ingredients are incorporated and smooth.

Add the flour. Mix on low speed until flour is no longer loose, then on medium speed until the flour is fully incorporated.

Line a cookie sheet with parchment paper. Using a medium-sized cookie scooper, scoop the cookie dough (approximately 2 tablespoons each) onto the cookie sheet, placing the scoops at least 2 inches apart.

Bake for 12 to 15 minutes, until the edges are browned and set.

Slide the parchment paper with cookies off the cookie sheet and directly onto the counter for cooling. (If not using parchment paper, let the cookies sit for 1 minute and then remove them to cool on the counter or a wire rack.) Sprinkle sanding sugar on top of the cookies.

Serve immediately and let all remaining cookies fully cool on the counter for at least 30 minutes before packaging into an airtight container. Packaging too soon will cause the cookies to soften and stick together.

I'm so glad that salt became a socially acceptable part of all of our desserts. I love a salty sweet, like a chocolate-covered pretzel, and I'll use any excuse to add a few grains of salt to the top of a chocolatey treat. This chocolate chip cookie is made with softened caramel bits spread throughout the dough. This makes for a chewy and undercooked texture that keeps you coming back for another bite.

SALTED CARAMEL COOKIES

PREP TIME: 10 MINUTES

BAKE TIME: 10 TO 13 MINUTES

MAKES 2 1/2 DOZEN COOKIES

1 cup (2 sticks) salted
    butter, softened
1 cup granulated white
    sugar
1/2 cup firmly packed light
    brown sugar
2 large eggs
2 teaspoons vanilla extract
1 teaspoon caramel extract
1 1/2 teaspoons salt
1/2 teaspoon baking soda
2 1/2 cups all-purpose flour
2/3 cup caramel bits
1 1/3 cup semisweet
    chocolate chips
1 tablespoon sea salt flakes,
    optional

Preheat the oven to 375 degrees.

In a large mixing bowl, cream the butter, white sugar, and brown sugar together using a hand/electric mixer on medium speed until the mixture is smooth.

Add the eggs, vanilla, caramel extract, salt, and baking soda to the butter mixture. Mix on medium speed until the ingredients are incorporated and smooth.

Add the flour. Mix on low speed until the flour is no longer loose, then on medium speed until the flour is fully incorporated.

Melt half of the caramel bits in the microwave for 30 seconds. Add the melted caramel bits and the remaining caramel bits into the dough until evenly mixed. Add the semisweet chocolate chips and mix on low speed until they are incorporated fully.

Line a cookie sheet with parchment paper. Using a medium-sized cookie scooper, scoop the cookie dough (approximately 2 tablespoons each) onto the cookie sheet, placing the scoops at least 2 inches apart.

Bake for 10 to 13 minutes, until the edges are browned and set.

Slide the parchment paper with cookies off the cookie sheet and directly onto the counter for cooling. (If not using parchment paper, let the cookies sit for 1 minute and then remove them to cool on the counter or a wire rack.)

If desired, before serving, sprinkle sea salt flakes onto cookies after they have cooled.

CHAPTER 4

BUILDING A BRAND

Tiff

Expanding a business and building a brand are two distinct enterprises. Expanding into new locations is more an effort of logistics, management, and perfecting of systems and processes to scale, while building a brand is the softer and harder-to-define art of creating meaning for customers. To us, creating a brand that resonates with our customers and becomes a meaningful and useful part of their lives is job number one. We figure that if we're able to accomplish that, everything else will fall into place. A lot goes into our branding, but three elements have become cornerstones of our brand: technology, charity, and warm moments.

TECHNOLOGY FIRST

Leon

We absolutely didn't set out to be a technology-first company. When we first started, we took all orders over the phone by pen and paper. But in the late '90s, websites were starting to become more commonplace, and we knew we needed to build one. We thought long and hard about what our web address should be, because we thought *tiffanystreats.com* would be too long and hard to understand. We came up with a bunch of ideas, but Tiff nailed it when she thought of *cookiedelivery.com*.

Since it was so early in the internet age, we snagged that URL and have used it as our website ever since. We were among the first brands to offer online ordering, with a rudimentary platform we launched in 2000. As we started to grow, our friends at the potato shop showed us how to enter call-in orders into QuickBooks, which wasn't ideal, but it was much better than pen and paper. The program allowed us to save some customer information, and we saw the efficiencies and advantages of having software. With the right software, we knew we had an opportunity to run better operations and provide an even better customer experience. We started looking at off-the-shelf software to see if anything already in the marketplace could work for our business.

Tiff

We took a demo of several order-taking software systems and plugged in our menu, but we couldn't make any of them work seamlessly. We were closest to a pizza delivery business since we did on-demand food delivery, but we also provided future ordering as well as gifting. No software handled all of those things, and the many workarounds required for our menu didn't save much time or work efficiently. Against the advice of some of our mentors, we decided we needed to build our own software. And so we met Phil.

I can't remember Phil's last name or how we found him; he's just a part of our history. For a reasonable price, he promised to build us custom software to input orders. Each week, we worked with him on our needs, and each time he'd come back with his progress. Until one day, Phil didn't show up. We called and called and left voicemails and emails, but no Phil. Eventually, we realized he'd ditched us. We termed it being "black-holed," as in "Phil black-holed us," meaning he was suddenly and mysteriously gone without a word, as if he had been sucked into a black hole in space, never to return. Today we'd say that Phil ghosted us.

What we came to realize—or at least to our best assumption—was that Phil was in over his head. He'd promised us a system for a price that was far too low, and our expectations and needs for the software outpaced what he could provide, especially for the price.

Post-Phil, we sought another solution. We found a company in India that would code software, and we worked remotely with them for a year, until we met roughly the same end. We weren't making enough headway, and where we needed to be didn't match the budget we had, so we parted ways.

This is the point where most people would give up and resign themselves to making an off-the-shelf solution work. We'd wasted two years and a bunch of money and had nothing to show for it. But we knew it needed to be done, and we were desperate to make it happen.

Third go-round, we hired a man who seemed professional and capable. Again, we worked with him regularly for months, frequently going to his apartment to review the newest build. Ultimately, we landed in the same place. It couldn't be done. The scope of the project was too great for an individual to do at this budget. He didn't ghost us, but he did sit us down and in no uncertain terms fired us as clients.

Suddenly, another opportunity presented itself. A good friend of ours who worked in the software industry introduced us to his coworker who, along with a partner, wanted to do some custom work on the side. This time, it wasn't a random find but a warm introduction to a trusted set of people. We sat down with them and instantly knew this process would be different. They looked at the project in another way, laying out the interface horizontally instead of vertically, as the other three developers had done. We began meeting weekly, and a year later, we finally debuted our custom order-taking software. That's all it did, but the system was built solely for us, so it worked smoothly. We knew this was the beginning of a new start.

Again, against the wisdom of the times, we made the unusual decision to make the software web-based. (Web-based software could be glitchy and slow, and what would we do if the site crashed or the internet went down?) This enabled us to begin remotely managing the store. We could oversee everything from anywhere.

We loved our new system, but we knew we were nowhere near done with it. There was so much more we wanted to do to help run the business and streamline operations! We continued to add features until the program ultimately became an enterprise solution for our business, with functions to integrate with payroll, HR, marketing, and more.

We use the same system but have continued to add to it and have invested over $15 million in our custom software. One of the original builders, Jocelyn, is our chief technology officer (CTO), and tech remains a huge focus for us. It enables us to enhance the customer experience and keep operations humming along as we grow. We even added an option for customers sending a gift delivery to include a video message, which plays in augmented reality on the box of cookies. It's called CookieVision, and we secured a patent for it.

We feel that starting the business in 1999 was perfect timing. To run a mom-and-pop delivery service, we relied on two major things: cell phones and the internet. Without those pieces of technology, it would have been difficult to start and get off the ground as easily as we did with the two of us. We've always seen technology as a founding structure to operating and growing our business and to creating a customer-friendly experience, and we lean into it every chance we get.

GIVING BACK

Leon

One of our greatest joys has been the ability to give back to the communities that support us. Throughout the years, we've worked with many nonprofit organizations and have given millions of dollars in cash, gift cards, and product as part of our mission to connect people through warm moments.

One of our favorite events is our Grand Opening, where we sell one dozen cookies at a discounted price and donate 100 percent of the sales to a charity. In the past, we've worked with numerous amazing charities, including the Make-A-Wish Foundation, where we'll sponsor a Wish Kid. For those events, we usually rent a limo and have it pick up our Wish Kid and their family at their home and drive them to the event, where the lines of customers clap and cheer. The Wish Kid then comes into the kitchen and helps us make and sell cookies to the crowd, all of it benefitting their wish. The joy in these children's faces, as they get a reprieve from their battle with a disease like cancer, is amazing to see.

Line wrapping around the building at our Arlington, Texas, Grand Opening charity event

We usually start the event on a Saturday at 9:00 a.m., with lines forming hours before the event start time. Our record for earliest line start was for our Grand Opening in Arlington, Texas, where the line started forming at 7:00 a.m. the Friday prior, twenty-six hours in advance! Lines for our Grand Openings usually wrap around the entire building and down the street.

These events, though fun, are hard work. The team often has to start baking at 4:00 a.m. to have enough cookies for the start of the event. We'll sell 1,500 dozen cookies or more in a few hours, so it's nonstop action. We used to staff these events only with salaried managers and corporate staff, so everyone working hard that day was volunteering their time to support the charity. It's still common to see our chief financial officer (CFO) helping bake the cookies, while our chief operating officer (COO) and our head of marketing package the cookies, and finance vice presidents work alongside store managers, handing out cookies and managing the line. We started this tradition for our third location in 2008 and have done a similar charity-based event for every store opening since.

We'd been doing these Grand Opening charity events for years when an opportunity came to raise money for a cause that hit close to home for us. A longtime employee, named Zach Medlin, was one of the many who'd started working as a delivery driver while in college, graduated, left, and returned in a different role after gaining outside experience. Zach had a cousin, Alexis, who with her husband, Peter, suffered the most immeasurable loss a human being can suffer: the death of their son, Connor, to DIPG (diffuse intrinsic pontine glioma), a rare childhood brain cancer.

When we opened a store in The Woodlands, where they lived, we wanted to do something special and picked their organization, the Connor Man Defeat DIPG Foundation, to support. We've never met a stronger couple than those two parents, who showed up at the event with smiling faces, determined to fund research for DIPG, in the hopes that other parents could be spared the pain they'd experienced. What we

Connor's family at our Grand Opening at The Woodlands

Alexis raising awareness for DIPG and the foundation

were able to contribute was a drop in the bucket, but since that event, we've connected with the DIPG network and continue to support various local charities for the same cause.

Tiff

In addition to these events for special occasions, every week our marketing team donates cookies to local charities and nonprofits, as part of our community giveback program. One of the first things we added to our website was the ability to request a donation online. We had so many people walk into the store who needed help with their nonprofits that we needed a way to organize the requests. The requests still pour in, and we love participating in all sorts of events, from giving cookies to children and nurses in the hospital on Christmas, to providing take-home cookies and gift cards at fundraising galas, to handing out congratulations cookies at the end of charity 5K races.

For both of us, giving back is something we'll always cherish. It's ingrained in our DNA, and our entire team rallies around being active in the community, helping to support important causes in a special way. I cried after the first several Grand Opening charity events we hosted, because I felt overwhelmed with gratitude that we were in a position to help even in a small way. It's been an unexpected blessing for us to be in that position, and we intend to continue using our brand to help however we can.

WARM MOMENTS

Leon

Lindsey, our Austin district manager, hung up the phone and looked at me with tears in her eyes. In a trembling voice she said, "I just took this order from a lady who is an admin at an office downtown. She was so happy when I said we could get the cookies out to her, still warm, in about an hour. She said it was an important order to her. Out of curiosity, I asked her what it was for, and she told me that the order was for her boss.

"On more than one occasion, on a rainy day, her boss would bring up how rainy days always reminded him fondly of his mother. When he was a child at school, any day it would rain, his mom had a tradition where she would bake him a batch of cookies he could enjoy when he got home. She went on to tell me that his mother recently passed away, and he has of course been sad about it.

"Well, today is the first day of rain since his mother has passed, so the whole office wanted to get together and order these cookies for him, in memory of his mother."

Lindsey and I sat there for a moment, both trying not to lose it. When she shared this story with the rest of the team, I felt this incredible sense of purpose fill the room.

When we started the business, we thought the mission was delivering warm cookies, baked fresh. There was a buzz of excitement around what we were doing, and we gave full credit to the novel concept and tasty product. However, a few years in, we started to see and hear from our customers. They'd call, email, and even write in with anecdotes about what Tiff's Treats has meant to them. We realized we weren't merely providing a service and product to people. We had a far more rewarding purpose: *we were connecting people through warm moments*. The cookies were a fun, convenient, and comforting conduit between people who wanted to express their love, gratitude, appreciation, sympathy, and more to friends, family, clients, and employees. What dawned on us was that every single day in our business, we get to see the best parts of human nature.

On days when we were struggling and fighting for the business's survival, these customer moments kept us going.

Tiff

One of the cool things about delivering warm moments is that we've created a business that's meaningful not only for Leon and me but also for our entire team. Working in a Tiff's Treats store is physically demanding; being on your feet hustling in a fast-paced environment day in and day out can be draining. Taking deliveries is equally stressful, dodging traffic as you work to get your orders to their destination on time without forgetting anything. But being greeted with smiles, knowing that what we're delivering brings joy and comfort to the customer, is so rewarding and inspires us on the busiest of days.

One of my favorite warm moments happened several years ago. Our Plano, Texas, store was receiving weekly orders for a six-year-old named Caleb, and each one had a countdown in the gift message. After many weeks of making these deliveries, the team finally found out what the countdown meant. Caleb had cancer and needed twenty chemo treatments. His grandparents were sending warm cookies from afar, counting down the treatments with their gift messages.

After a few weeks, the Plano store team joined the countdown. When we got to order zero, Chris, the store manager, couldn't help but call Caleb's mom and ask how he was doing. She was shocked to find out the whole store had been following along all those weeks, rooting for Caleb's recovery. When word came that Caleb's biopsy showed that he was cancer-free, the store erupted in celebration and sent the mom cookies, along with a $100 gift card and a note of congratulations.

I can't think of a bigger honor than to be a part of this encouragement and ultimate celebration. And as a parent myself, to know that strangers were rooting for my son and joining in on the journey . . . I can only imagine that would make it all the sweeter.

These moments of connection have built the brand for us. Our job is to take our responsibility seriously and make every decision based on the knowledge that we're providing something meaningful to customers. Hundreds of special moments have come our way, and throughout the book, you'll see some of our favorites sprinkled in, so you can share in the love we're privileged to witness. Perhaps most importantly in our evolution, these warm moments served as the springboard for us becoming a values-driven brand.

Leon loves banana nut bread, and this cookie has always been one of his favorites; he insists that we offer it every year. The stores don't love it as much. The dough is sticky and hard to work with, and the bananas go bad fast, so the shelf life is short. But that won't matter to you, since these will all be eaten right away. The banana creates a fluffier texture that's almost bread-like but packs a sweet cookie flavor.

BANANA NUT COOKIES

PREP TIME: 10 MINUTES
BAKE TIME: 10 TO 12 MINUTES
MAKES 2 1/2 DOZEN COOKIES

- 1 cup (2 sticks) salted butter, softened
- 1 cup granulated white sugar
- 1/2 cup firmly packed light brown sugar
- 2 large eggs
- 2 teaspoons vanilla extract
- 1 1/2 teaspoons salt
- 1/2 teaspoon baking soda
- 2 1/3 cups all-purpose flour
- 1 whole yellow banana
- 1 1/2 cups chopped walnuts

Preheat the oven to 375 degrees.

In a large mixing bowl, cream the butter, white sugar, and brown sugar together using a hand/electric mixer on medium speed until the mixture is smooth.

Add the eggs, vanilla, salt, and baking soda to the butter mixture. Mix on medium speed until the ingredients are incorporated and smooth.

Add the flour. Mix on low speed until the flour is no longer loose, then on medium speed until the flour is fully incorporated.

Peel and mash 1 whole banana with a potato masher. Add the mashed banana and chopped walnuts to the dough and mix on low speed until everything is evenly combined.

Line a cookie sheet with parchment paper. Using a medium-sized cookie scooper, scoop the cookie dough (approximately 2 table-spoons each) onto the cookie sheet, placing the scoops at least 2 inches apart.

Bake for 10 to 12 minutes, until the edges are browned and set.

Slide the parchment paper with cookies off the cookie sheet and directly onto the counter for cooling. (If not using parchment paper, let the cookies sit for 1 minute and then remove them to cool on the counter or on a wire rack.)

Serve warm.

Chocolate bar pieces, along with tiny marshmallows and graham crackers for extra flavor, make this one a nostalgic summertime treat—all of the summer vacation vibes and none of the blackened marshmallows that are somehow cold in the center. (I am not good at roasting marshmallows.) When we made the first batch of these cookies, I pulled one apart, and behold: the marshmallow stretches out, just like a Rice Krispies Treat! The delightfully sticky and chewy texture sets it apart from your standard cookie, making you beg for s'more. Okay, that was too far, but you get what I'm saying here.

S'MORES COOKIES

PREP TIME: 10 MINUTES

BAKE TIME: 10 TO 13 MINUTES

MAKES 3 DOZEN COOKIES

. . . .

1 (7-ounce) giant milk
    chocolate bar
5 full graham crackers
    (4 small rectangles
    each), crushed (about 1
    1/4 cups)
1 1/8 cups (2 1/4 sticks) salted
    butter, softened
1 cup granulated white
    sugar
1/2 cup firmly packed light
    brown sugar
2 large eggs
2 teaspoons vanilla extract
1 1/2 teaspoons salt
1/2 teaspoon baking soda
2 1/4 cups all-purpose flour
1 (3-ounce) package vanilla
    marshmallow bits

Preheat the oven to 375 degrees.

Break the milk chocolate bar into small pieces by hand (each rectangle into approximately 8 pieces) and set aside.

Break the graham crackers into small pieces by hand and set aside.

In a large mixing bowl, cream the butter, white sugar, and brown sugar together using a hand/electric mixer on medium speed until the mixture is smooth.

Add the eggs, vanilla, salt, and baking soda to the butter mixture. Mix on medium speed until the ingredients are incorporated and smooth.

Add the flour. Mix on low speed until the flour is no longer loose, then on medium speed until the flour is fully incorporated.

Add the milk chocolate bar pieces, graham cracker pieces, and vanilla marshmallow bits, and mix on low speed until incorporated fully. If all ingredients aren't evenly distributed, follow up with hand mixing.

Line a cookie sheet with parchment paper. Using a medium-sized cookie scooper, scoop the cookie dough (approximately 2 tablespoons each) onto the cookie sheet, placing the scoops at least 2 inches apart.

Bake for 10 to 13 minutes, until the edges are browned and set.

Slide the parchment paper with cookies off the cookie sheet and directly onto the counter for cooling. (If not using parchment paper, let the cookies sit for 1 minute and then remove them to cool on the counter or a wire rack.)

Serve warm.

Warm Moment

Dear Tiff's Treats Team,

Thank you for coming over to talk with my mom and me at the opening on Saturday. You put on a great event. My mom was so happy your staff used her bears we brought to donate on the main table. It meant the world to her for a reason we have not shared with you until now.

Friday was two months to the day my stepdad passed away. My parents joined me for the first time at a grand opening and came to your Arlington store. My dad loved your cookies and your store concept. We got there around four in the morning and had no idea Arlington would turn out so many people so early compared to the Fort Worth West 7th store, when I originally met you at 5:00 a.m. We stayed anyway and were forty-two, forty-three, and forty-four in line. We bought eighteen dozen between the three of us and always donated a gift. We had fun spending time together, talking and laughing while waiting for the doors to open. I don't know if you remember my dad—he was the one in the motorized purple chair. (He loved TCU [Texas Christian University].) When I was loading my parents up to leave, Dad began to not feel well. Leon came by and said thanks for coming. My folks left to run some errands, and I went back home.

Later that day, we lost Dad to a sudden heart attack. They had made it home safely in their driveway, and my dad sent my mom into their house to check on the dog. He didn't want to worry her. He said he was tired and wanted to sit there in the van for a second before he went in. When Mom came back out with their dog, Dad looked at my mom and informed her he had called 911. Neither the ambulance nor hospital could revive him. Mom lost her partner in life and lost the man who raised me.

My mom and I are thankful we got the opportunity to spend that morning as a family. We truly enjoyed being together. This is the main reason Mom wanted to do it again at Southlake then travel to Lewisville. My mom will be seventy next month. That being said, she was determined to go, and we got there around 2:00 a.m. Mom got to know several of the folks around us in line; it's just her outgoing nature. We braved the chilly night and the seven hours till 9:00 a.m. And it was all worth it! Again, she was happy her teddy bears were on display on the main table. You were kind and wonderful as usual. We left to drive to Lewisville and on the way home, we reminisced about Dad and how he would have enjoyed the openings. We know he was watching and loving it all. My dad passed away at the age of sixty-eight. His father, my step-granddad, passed on at the age of fifty-seven—both of heart disease. He had a flair for life and never met a stranger . . .

My folks would drive in from North Richland Hills to get a box of cookies and the occasional brownie. Dad's favorite was your chocolate chip pecan. We miss him every day, but we remember the happy times we spent together. Tiff's Treats holds a special place in our hearts and always will.

—David Tucker

CHAPTER 5

THE TIFF'S TOP FIVE

Tiff

One day many years ago, we set a meeting where the topic was how to "bottle it." We wanted to figure out how to capture the magic we were creating at Tiff's Treats, so we could take it anywhere and create the same magic all over the country. But that meant we'd have to understand what we were doing and commit it to paper.

We sat down with our leadership team and set out to do just that. What came out of that meeting was a written list of the values we'd been operating by without even knowing it. As it turns out, we're a values-driven brand. We didn't start by creating a company based on a shared set of values that would steer us. Quite the opposite. We created a company to sell cookies. But over time, our customers and our team began educating us on what the company meant to them, and we realized we were running by an unofficial set of values.

We named these values "Tiff's Top Five," and over the course of a few years, we weaved them into the fabric of our corporate vocabulary. From delivery drivers to managers to admins and executives, every day you'll hear a Top Five listed as a reason to do (or not do) something. We even created an orientation course for all new hires that revolves around these values. Whether you're working at a store in the kitchen or you're our new COO, you sit in this class together and learn about what's important to us at Tiff's Treats. If it resonates with you, great, and welcome! And if not, no problem—but this is the time to part ways.

By no means are these the only values that are important to us, but as they're aptly named, these are our Top Five.

#1: WE MAKE PEOPLE HAPPY

Leon

At the core of what we do, *we connect people through warm moments*. People rely on us to be a part of special moments in their lives. When we meet new people and they hear we started Tiff's Treats, the first thing they usually do is share their "warm moment," their first or favorite Tiff's Treats experience. The comment we've received most often over the years goes something like this:

"I'll never forget the first time I had Tiff's Treats! My husband and I had our first baby and were in the hospital. My sister-in-law sends over a box of warm cookies, so we're sitting on our hospital bed at the end of a crazy day, holding our brand-new baby and a box of Tiff's Treats, and it was the best moment ever. We loved it so much, whenever our friends or family have babies, we send Tiff's Treats to the hospital."

We love this because it's extremely rare for any brand to be able to participate in one of the best moments of someone's life, like the birth of a child. Few brands get to be part of something so amazing and personal, but for some reason, our brand does. That is truly special and something we don't ever want to take for granted.

Tiff

It's not only those special occasion moments either. Part of what makes us unique is that it's socially acceptable to order Tiff's Treats for yourself as much as it would be to send Tiff's Treats as a gift to someone. We're there to celebrate the highs—births, anniversaries, weddings, promotions—and also to provide comfort in the lows—deaths, illnesses, and loss. And while we've been a part of some truly incredible, impactful moments, we also make people happy as a regular part of their daily lives. We have as many people ordering a box of warm cookies to share with family, friends, or coworkers for no special occasion, but we get to be the highlight of their day. Many people go in on an order at the office on a Friday afternoon, or maybe over the weekend with their families. While these orders aren't for a specific celebration, we've found that sharing a warm cookie provides a moment of connection and joy.

#2: WE MAKE IT RIGHT

Leon

Because we're involved in so many "moments," it's important that we "make it right," no matter the situation. In the business of on-demand delivery and on-demand gifting, we're bound to make mistakes. We try hard to minimize them, but it still happens. We have a company goal to keep our error rate to 0.35 percent or under, which means we strive to be accurate 99.65 percent of the time. Even when the mistake isn't our fault, we strive to make it right.

An example of this would be when somebody places an online order to a business client in suite 300, but the customer accidentally types in suite 200 during the online ordering process. Invariably, we'll deliver to the wrong place. Throughout the years, we've found that if we accidentally deliver to the next-door neighbors, *even with the name of their neighbor on the outside of the box*, the cookies never make it to the right person—they will, 100 percent of the time, get eaten! It's kind of a weird social experiment on honesty, when you see people who are probably honest 99 percent of the time eat cookies that are accidentally delivered to them, even if they know where the cookies should go.

If this situation does happen, and the customer who ordered the gift calls back and asks where the order is, our team knows to "make it right" by remaking the order and sending it out for free. Many times, the customer will realize they entered the wrong suite number, but one of our values is to *overdeliver* and make sure the customer gets what they intended to get—in this case, a gift delivery to the proper recipient.

Tiff

We've found this value to be helpful for our team. Before we had "We Make It Right" as a concrete value, our managers would often get upset when having to remake an order. Even though this had no repercussion for them, they had angst over who was at fault. Having this value on the wall means it doesn't matter who was at fault. What matters is that the customer expected to have a certain experience, and if they didn't get that experience for whatever reason, it's our job to make it right.

This helps with our customer service team as well. When a disappointed customer calls, our staff doesn't have to put the customer on hold to try to figure out what they are and are not allowed to do. They know the goal: make it right. This almost always means redelivering the order, so we can attempt to recapture the magic the customer hoped to create the first time, as well as offering something extra for their trouble.

How many times have we all had a bad delivery experience and were offered only a refund or a credit? Neither of those offers helps correct today's problem, yet these are the go-to make-good tactics for so many companies. We certainly bear a financial cost associated with this philosophy, but we've found that if customers are entrusting us with their special moments, they want to know that we'll have their back if something goes wrong. Creating trust with customers is one of our most important values, and we credit this commitment for creating an especially loyal customer base.

#3: WE PROTECT THE BRAND

Leon

Protecting the brand is something we regularly talk about within the organization. It only recently dawned on me that when we're talking about "protecting the brand," we're actually talking about protecting it from *ourselves* more than anything else. When we were small and struggling, we never had a myriad of choices in what we could do. We usually had *one* option, and we had to execute that option the best we could. As we've grown and seen some success as a business, different options start opening up for the business, and that's not necessarily a good thing if a values filter isn't in place.

In the beginning, Tiff and I weren't great at many things, but we knew what we wanted Tiff's Treats to be and focused all of our energy and effort on that. We didn't know or understand what we were doing until we read a business book by Jim Collins, *Good to Great*. In the book he talks about his Hedgehog Concept, which is focusing on what a company can be *best in the world* at. When we read that, it resonated with us. We invented the warm-cookie delivery industry and pioneered the on-demand gifting industry. We feel we are best in the world at that and intend to remain so. Inspired by Collins's Hedgehog Concept, we doubled down on making sure that we only did things that were in service of being "best in the world" at what we do.

Over the years, we've remained relatively simple in how we operate and what we provide as far as product and service. We're careful when adding to our product offerings, which must be in service of, and not a distraction from, being best in the world at warm-cookie delivery. This doesn't mean we avoid expanding our offerings. We've branched out to serving other treats aligned with our mission, such as decadent brownie and blondie bars (The Tiff's Trio®), a blended ice cream treat (the Tiffblitz®), cookie truffles, Tiff's Treats Take and Bake® (our shipped cookie dough kit), and more. But staying laser-focused on what we do best has been a key to our growth. We use "protect the brand" as our filter, whether it's at the store level or the board level.

#4: WE ARE PASSIONATE

Leon

This one comes from a conversation we had years ago with two people on our leadership team, Jocelyn Seever and Kullen Kifer. Kullen was one of our first delivery drivers while he was in college. When he graduated, he left for a corporate job, got an MBA, and then came back to be our CFO. Jocelyn is our CTO. She's the architect of our entire technology stack and, as previously mentioned, built our proprietary system.

Both Jocelyn and Kullen landed high-paying careers with big companies after college. Yet they both wound up at Tiff's Treats, working double the hours while getting paid half of what they were used to making. The company was young when they joined us, and we didn't have the sales to pay them market rate. I remember working with them in the conference room on a particularly stressful day, and looking over at them, bewildered that we somehow suckered these two incredible talents into working at Tiff's Treats. I couldn't help it and said to them, "Hey, Tiff and I are beyond grateful we have you two here with us growing this brand. But I have to ask you: What in the world were you guys thinking? You both had such successful starts to your careers in the corporate world. I don't want to lose you, but I have to know why you guys are even here when you obviously could be making more money elsewhere."

They both had the same sentiment. Kullen said, "We're here because we want to be part of something that is bigger than ourselves. We have a chance to do something that has never been done before—we get to build an entire industry from scratch together. That isn't an opportunity that comes along every day." Jocelyn nodded her head in agreement.

From that moment, Tiff and I understood. It has since been a rallying cry for anyone who joins our organization. Walking down the halls of our office, you'll see wonderful people who are here because they want the same thing: to make history, to build something that has never been built before. We talk about it often with our team and have realized it's such an intrinsic motivating factor. So we hire people who have a passion around building and creating something special together.

#5: WE ADAPT AND GROW

Tiff

In my experience, there are two kinds of people: those who are uncomfortable with change and those who hate it. That's not entirely true, but it's safe to say that change is an unsettling concept for most people, which is why it's one of our values. If change is something you can't get on board with, and you're hoping for a job that remains basically the same from your first day to your last, you're in the wrong place. Starting a company in a nonexistent industry means you get used to adapting things to fit your needs and making changes when something better comes along.

Baking cookies on demand, to order, is not how bakery equipment is designed to be used. Typically, bakeries bake large batches of goodies, let them cool, and sell them later. To bake an individual order, package the cookies hot, and deliver them immediately means we've had to adapt our equipment and tools. For example, one timer for an oven full of cookies doesn't work if you're baking each rack at a different time.

Technology is also a big source of change. Since the first day, we've used technology to make our business run, and we update our platform regularly and look for newer and better systems to tie into as they become available. Operationally, we're always striving to improve, and we often implement new processes to better support being best in the world at warm-cookie delivery. In one year alone, we documented over one hundred process changes to operations!

However, there's a balance, and we've found that while adapting is vital to growth, it must be tempered with an amount of change that people can absorb and enact effectively. (Spoiler alert: one hundred changes is too many.) In any case, whether you like change or hate it, it's exciting to work in a place that is always striving toward improvement. Our jobs are never the same year to year or even day to day, and that makes twenty-plus years at the same job as fun as day one.

· · ·

Leon

Over the years, we joked that by reviewing Tiff's Top Five at the beginning when someone joined our team, we at least gave them fair warning as to what we were about ahead of time. If they didn't like what they saw in the Top Five, they wouldn't succeed here and probably shouldn't stay in the job.

A couple of years ago, one of our Tiff's Top Five instructors was in a conference room with a group of new hires, going over the Top Five. In the middle of the orientation, one of the new delivery drivers stood up, slammed his hands on the table, said, "F*** this—I'm out," and walked out of the room. When Tiff and I were told about this, we were delighted to hear that someone had enough self-awareness to know they weren't a fit for us and vice versa. Thanks to the Tiff's Top Five, this person saved himself and the company a lot of wasted time, energy, and frustration.

Tiff

In the early days of the business, we operated by instinct and struggled to communicate what we thought made us special. And as we began expanding to more locations in different cities, we feared that we'd lose our culture as we grew, and our team wouldn't be ambassadors for what was important to us. Though "bottling up magic" might not have been an attainable goal, committing to a set of values—Tiff's Top Five—has been a helpful guide in uniting the entire team in our common purpose to spread joy and comfort, through warm cookie moments across the country.

I was twenty-three when I first discovered red velvet cake. I don't know how it escaped me before then, but it was a pleasant surprise to find out that red-colored cake was chocolate and topped with cream cheese frosting, which had not escaped me and has always been one of my favorite frostings. Why is it red? I don't know, but it does make for an elegant-looking dessert. We put cream cheese inside the dough and top the cookies with powdered sugar. We generally run this flavor in January because it feels wintry to me, like something you should eat with a cup of hot chocolate in a big faux fur coat. I don't have a coat like that, but if I did, I'm certain I'd be eating Red Velvet Cookies.

RED VELVET COOKIES

PREP TIME: 10 MINUTES

BAKE TIME: 10 TO 12 MINUTES

MAKES 2 1/2 DOZEN COOKIES

- 1 1/8 cups (2 1/4 sticks) salted butter, softened
- 3 ounces cream cheese
- 2 tablespoons sour cream
- 1 cup granulated white sugar
- 5/8 cup firmly packed light brown sugar
- 2 large eggs
- 2 teaspoons vanilla extract
- 1 1/2 teaspoons salt
- 1/2 teaspoon baking soda
- 1/2 tablespoon red food coloring
- 1 1/2 tablespoons distilled white vinegar
- 2 1/3 cups all-purpose flour
- 1/4 cup HERSHEY'S Special Dark Dutch Cocoa
- 1 cup powdered sugar

Preheat the oven to 375 degrees.

In a large mixing bowl, cream the butter, cream cheese, sour cream, white sugar, and brown sugar together using a hand/electric mixer on medium speed until the mixture is smooth.

Add the eggs, vanilla, salt, baking soda, red food coloring, and distilled white vinegar to the butter mixture. Mix on medium speed until the ingredients are incorporated and smooth.

Add the flour and cocoa. Mix on low speed until the flour is no longer loose, then on medium speed until the flour is fully incorporated.

Line a cookie sheet with parchment paper. Using a medium-sized cookie scooper, scoop the cookie dough (approximately 2 tablespoons each) onto the cookie sheet, placing the scoops at least 2 inches apart.

Bake for 10 to 12 minutes, until the tops and edges are set.

Slide the parchment paper with cookies off the cookie sheet and directly onto the counter for cooling. (If not using parchment paper, let the cookies sit for 1 minute and then remove them to cool on the counter or a wire rack.)

Before serving, sprinkle powdered sugar onto the cookies after they have cooled.

Notes:
Add a few additional drops of red food coloring for darker red-colored cookies.

Using standard unsweetened cocoa instead of HERSHEY'S Special Dark Dutch Cocoa will result in a lighter-colored dough with a less-rich chocolate flavor.

Just like the ice cream, this is a chocolate cookie with marshmallows and almonds mixed in. We use two kinds of marshmallows here. Freeze-dried marshmallow bits hold their shape for visual appeal, while the mini marshmallows melt and create a kind of sticky glaze, which adds depth to the flavor and texture of the cookie. Because of employee demand, Rocky Road was added to our Flavor of the Week lineup. We ran it once many years ago and then forgot about it until several newer employees asked if we'd ever make a Rocky Road Cookie. We already had, so we dusted off the recipe and brought it back to life.

ROCKY ROAD COOKIES

PREP TIME: 10 MINUTES

BAKE TIME: 9 TO 11 MINUTES

MAKES 2 $1/2$ DOZEN COOKIES

- 1 cup (2 sticks) salted butter, softened
- 1 cup granulated white sugar
- $1/2$ cup firmly packed light brown sugar
- 2 large eggs
- 2 teaspoons vanilla extract
- $1 1/2$ teaspoons salt
- $1/2$ teaspoon baking soda
- 2 cups all-purpose flour
- $1/4$ cup HERSHEY'S Special Dark Dutch Cocoa
- 1 tablespoon milk
- 5.5 ounces milk chocolate chips
- $1 1/2$ cups sliced blanched almonds
- 1 (3-ounce) package vanilla marshmallows bits
- $1/2$ cup mini marshmallows (frozen for a few hours for best results)

Preheat the oven to 375 degrees.

In a large mixing bowl, cream the butter, white sugar, and brown sugar together using a hand/electric mixer on medium speed until the mixture is smooth.

Add the eggs, vanilla, salt, and baking soda to the butter mixture. Mix on medium speed until the ingredients are incorporated and smooth.

Add the flour, cocoa, and milk. Mix on low speed until the flour is no longer loose, then on medium speed until the flour is fully incorporated.

Add the chocolate chips, almonds, and vanilla marshmallow bits and mix on low speed until the ingredients are incorporated fully. Lightly fold the mini marshmallows into the dough by hand until evenly mixed.

Line a cookie sheet with parchment paper. Using a medium-sized cookie scooper, scoop the cookie dough (approximately 2 tablespoons each) onto the cookie sheet, placing the scoops at least 2 inches apart.

Bake for 9 to 11 minutes, until the tops and edges are set.

Slide the parchment paper with cookies off the cookie sheet and directly onto the counter for cooling. (If not using parchment paper, let the cookies sit for 1 minute and then remove them to cool on the counter or a wire rack.)

Serve warm.

Note: Using standard unsweetened cocoa instead of HERSHEY'S Special Dark Dutch Cocoa will result in a lighter-colored dough with a less-rich chocolate flavor.

Warm Moment

An order came in for a man in Nashville who was on his deathbed in a hospital. His last wish was for Blue Bell Ice Cream. Since we carry Blue Bell, our driver delivered a pint and a box of cookies. The driver shared the following:

"At first, I couldn't get a hold of the lady who ordered. She finally came out of the ward, and I think she needed a hug. Got the ice cream and mentioned it, and she cried and hugged me for a while. She said that she thought her grandpa would probably pass away that afternoon, and they always used to share Blue Bell together. She was super thankful. Just said thanks for making some of his last moments with us memorable."

While the Blue Bell Ice Cream was the memory between a dying grandfather and his granddaughter, it was a moment that we made possible, along with a box of warm cookies.

CHAPTER 6
OUR LOVE STORY

Tiff

It was ninth grade, and we'd been classmates for a few years. Aware of each other, yes, but neither of us particularly fond of the other. One thing we agreed on: we hated each other's shoes—mine a pair of preppy loafers and his a pair of oversized basketball shoes. When we entered high school the next year, we became fast friends through a shared theater class. We had a bonding moment when we both bombed on stage with a particularly bad rendition of a scene from *Last of the Red Hot Lovers*.

From there our friendship grew, and so did the number of times Leon asked me out. We went on a few dates but mostly remained friends throughout high school. We attended prom together as friends and even went so far as to buy an iconic best friends' necklace, where we each wore half of the medallion.

Leon's version of that story is that we were a couple when we went to prom, but we're happy to agree to disagree on that point.

Leon throwing Tiff a surprise birthday party in high school

Leon

I remember Tiff from ninth grade, and her goofy-looking leather loafers with tassels. She is exactly five feet tall, but she had the lowest voice, at least an octave lower than mine. I asked her out probably ten times in high school, with her occasionally saying yes. The rest of the time, she'd tell me that she didn't want to date. But I persisted, partly because every so often she'd say or do something that made me think I had a chance. I was always drawn to her humor and her

Prom night 1997!

smarts and, of course, I thought she was cute. It wasn't love at first sight for either of us, but I had a major crush on her far before it was reciprocated.

I was living on my own partway through my sophomore year of high school while both of my parents, who were divorced, separately worked overseas. They were out of the country for multiple Thanksgivings and Christmases while I was in high school. Tiff always invited me to spend the holidays with her and her family.

It's corny to admit this, but I already knew I loved her back then. We went to prom as friends, but absolutely emerged from prom a couple, though Tiff denies it. Our first kiss was at prom, and we went on dates after that. The conversation still gets contentious when we discuss when we actually started dating.

Tiff

The summer after we graduated from high school, we had a falling out. Leon was tired of waiting for me to commit to dating him, so he moved on, got a new girlfriend, and tried to avoid me. Which left me pretty lonely, since even then most of our friends were shared and were spending time with him instead of with me. I was traveling for my summer job anyway, so we would've spent the summer apart regardless.

Leon

By "falling out" she means she didn't want to date me that summer, even though I foolishly thought after prom, we'd at least have a summer romance. She made it clear that there'd be none of that. Brokenhearted, I knew I needed to move on, so I started dating someone else that summer. I truly thought that our relationship would end there.

I now understand where Tiff was coming from. I'd always had this massive thing for her and casually dating never would have satisfied me. For her, we had moments when we experienced a real connection, but she knew if it continued, it would have been a serious relationship at a time when she wasn't ready for one.

Tiff

The following fall, we both enrolled at the University of Texas at Austin. I was there a few weeks early and on my calendar had circled Leon's arrival date and phone number. On his first day there, I promptly called him and invited myself over. I knew he was dating someone else, but I was anxious to see him again. I'd missed our friendship.

During those first few months of college, his new relationship fizzled out, while our friendship started to turn romantic. We lived in dorms that were right down the street from each other, and I'd walk over to see him almost every day. Soon enough, we officially became a couple. He even once referred to me as "his wife" in front of his roommates after having had a few too many drinks.

Fast-forward one year. We were boyfriend and girlfriend, and we hit the infamous "date" where I stood him up. As we said earlier, it was more of an agreed-upon time to hang out than an actual date, but a simple text to let him know I was running late would have averted the whole mess. But that was 1999. I didn't have a cell phone, and texting wouldn't be invented for many more years. And so we launched an entire business—an entirely new industry—over a scheduling mishap.

For the next year, we went to school during the day and ran the business together at night. As we neared our junior year of college, we had an unusual epiphany. We'd only ever been in a serious relationship with each other, and it didn't seem to be ending anytime soon. So we did what any happy couple would do: we scheduled our breakup.

In true rom-com style, on January 1, 2000, we would break off our romantic relationship so that we could spend the last half of our college years single and able to meet other people. We figured that college was the best time to meet new people and not be tied down.

New Year's Eve that year was a memorable one—the turn of the millennium and also the last day we'd be a couple. Plus, we didn't know if Y2K was a thing and if all the stoplights and civilization as a whole would end at midnight. (It didn't.) The next day arrived as scheduled, and I spent January 1 feeling sad and worried that we'd made the wrong choice. In any case, we stuck with it.

For the next two years, we spent all of our afternoons and evenings together working on the business, but largely spent the weekends (when the business was closed) with our own friends. We were single-ish, and it worked about as well as you'd expect. Neither of us ever had another relationship; we were together too much for that to happen. But we spent plenty of time hurting each other in the process of dating other people.

Leon

In hindsight, the breakup idea was a terrible one. We were mature enough to know we needed to date other people but not mature enough to handle any of it with grace. There were awkward moments and a lot of jealousy, and it's amazing the situation didn't tank the business. Some way and somehow, we barreled through and did what we could to focus on the business during those last eighteen months of college.

Tiff

After we graduated from college, we had a big decision to make: Should we continue with the business or toss it all aside and get regular jobs? We'd invested so much into running the business and so little into school (we both came out with degrees, but few skills to speak of). We made the natural choice to go full-time with the business. We worked day and night, spending all of our time together, just the two of us.

Gradually, over the next few years, we became a couple again, although we never discussed it. Dating anyone else would have been impossible, unless that date happened in the store, since that's where we spent every minute.

One day, we drove past a storage facility, and I tossed out this idea: *If I put my things in storage, I could move into your apartment, and we'd save half on rent.* It made sense. We spent all of our time at the store, and any time at home was either spent sleeping or being alone, when the other one of us was at work.

So that's exactly what we did. I moved my things into storage and kept just enough to fill one drawer in his dresser and one drawer in his bathroom. We lived that way for a year, in his five-hundred-square-foot apartment on the bottom floor (underground actually), which tended to grow mold in the bathroom. It was eye-opening to realize that two drawers provided plenty of space for everything I needed.

When I turned twenty-four, Leon got me the best birthday present I've ever received: a six-week-old puppy for us to share. His name was Buster, and we were instantly in love with him. After six months of him chewing up the carpet and using every square inch of that apartment as a toilet, I realized he needed a house with a backyard. I again had a sensible idea: *If I bought a house, would you move there with*

Our first baby, Buster

me and pay rent for a room? I couldn't afford it alone. Leon said yes, so I set off to find us a house. My grandmother had recently divided up her remaining nest egg, and each grandchild had gotten a bit of money. I used my $6,000 on a down payment for a small house. In those days,

they were giving out mortgages to practically anyone for any amount— even me, whose income was nearly nonexistent. You didn't need much, or any, down payment, so within a few months we had ourselves a house!

Leon

Buster ultimately brought us back together. We loved that dog and treated him like a child. I joke that because we didn't have to send Buster out into the real world, like we'd have to do with our human

Our first home!

children, we were able to spoil him way more than we'd ever spoil our twins. Raising Buster together made it feel like we already had a family unit. To share so much love for something else, together, was special and a turning point in our relationship.

Buster as "best dog" in our wedding

Our sweet Buster came into our lives when we were twenty-four years old, when the business was just getting started. He lived 16.5 years, through the growth of the business, our marriage (serving as "best dog" in the wedding), the birth of our twins—every special life moment. It was and is terribly sad not to have him in our lives, but we'll always be grateful for him being the catalyst for our relationship and the family we have today.

Tiff

After seven years of living together in that house, we finally got married. We were busy building the business and needed time to save up money to afford a wedding. Friend after friend would meet someone and get married, leaving us the longest tenured but unmarried couple. This didn't bother us much. We were happy with our status quo.

We planned the wedding around our busy season. We selected a non-Capitol session year (Capitol season brought in big orders) and made sure to wait until after Mother's Day and National Chocolate Chip Day, of course. We had a beautiful wedding, attended by family and friends, as well as all of our board members and even Dr. and Mrs. Schneider, the landlords of our first store. It was a special time, when all of our business contacts were becoming people we considered family.

It took a minute to get used to being officially married. We'd been "together," but not married, for so long that the status was practically part of our identity. Right after our wedding ceremony ended, a server at the reception approached me and asked what I'd like to drink and what my husband would like to drink. I immediately answered with my knee-jerk response: "Oh, he's not my husband," which must have been quite confusing to this woman who'd just witnessed us saying our vows.

Since we met each other at such a young age, we have a longer love story than many. There's something extra special about knowing exactly what your spouse looked like and acted like at twelve years old, eighteen years old, twenty-five years old, and so on. If nothing else, it's certainly good blackmail material.

The number of life stages we've gone through together and the amount of memories we've made during those times add to our appreciation of each other. We literally and figuratively have grown up with the other person right by our side. And while our romantic relationship has been punctuated with practical decision after practical decision, somehow, when we weren't paying attention, we created a whole life for ourselves. A life which now includes a set of twins, a boy and a girl. And Leon and I are still best friends. We even have the necklaces to prove it.

Getting married

This cookie has such a light and bright flavor that it's hard to eat just one. They're like the potato chips of cookies in that way. We usually run Lemon Sugar Cookies in the spring or summer, but they're a customer favorite and requested year-round. You don't have to be a lemon lover to enjoy this one. The flavor is more mild than tart and can be a great starter treat for developing a taste for lemon-flavored desserts.

LEMON SUGAR COOKIES

PREP TIME: 10 MINUTES

BAKE TIME: 9 TO 11 MINUTES

MAKES 2 1/2 DOZEN COOKIES

- 1 1/8 cups (2 1/4 sticks) salted butter, softened
- 1 cup granulated white sugar
- 1/2 cup firmly packed light brown sugar
- 2 large eggs
- 1 teaspoon vanilla extract
- 1 1/2 teaspoons salt
- 1/2 teaspoon baking soda
- 1 1/4 teaspoons lemon extract
- 2 1/4 cups all-purpose flour
- 1/2 cup powdered sugar

Preheat the oven to 375 degrees.

In a large mixing bowl, cream the butter, white sugar, and brown sugar together using a hand/electric mixer on medium speed until the mixture is smooth.

Add the eggs, vanilla, salt, and baking soda to the butter mixture. Mix on medium speed until the ingredients are incorporated and smooth.

Whisk in the lemon extract.

Add the flour. Mix on low speed until the flour is no longer loose, then on medium speed until the flour is fully incorporated.

Line a cookie sheet with parchment paper. Using a medium-sized cookie scooper, scoop the cookie dough (approximately 2 tablespoons each) onto the cookie sheet, placing the scoops at least 2 inches apart.

Bake for 9 to 11 minutes, until the edges are browned and set.

Slide the parchment paper with cookies off the cookie sheet and directly onto the counter for cooling. (If not using parchment paper, let the cookies sit for 1 minute and then remove them to cool on the counter or a wire rack.)

Before serving and once cooled, sprinkle powdered sugar over the cookies for topping.

A friend once served me a dessert of a raspberry stuffed with a semisweet chocolate chip. I loved that combination, and I wanted to create a cookie that captured it. I have one cardinal rule, though, when it comes to fruit: I will not use dried fruit in cookies (raisins are the one exception). Dried fruit doesn't taste good in cookies, so those cookies don't sell. We finally landed on a method using fresh raspberries. The cookies come out pink, which is a bit unusual, and fluffier than normal, but the flavor is fresh and vibrant. Generally, I like to underbake my cookies, but these hold up best if they're cooked all the way through.

RASPBERRY CHOCOLATE COOKIES

PREP TIME: 10 MINUTES

BAKE TIME: 13 TO 16 MINUTES

MAKES 2 $\frac{1}{2}$ TO 3 DOZEN
    COOKIES

. . . .

1 cup (2 sticks) salted
    butter, softened
1 cup granulated white
    sugar
$\frac{1}{2}$ cup firmly packed light
    brown sugar
1 $\frac{1}{2}$ cups fresh raspberries
2 large eggs
2 teaspoons vanilla extract
1 $\frac{1}{2}$ teaspoons salt
$\frac{1}{2}$ teaspoon baking soda
2 $\frac{1}{3}$ cups all-purpose flour
1 cup semisweet chocolate
    chips

Preheat the oven to 375 degrees.

In a large mixing bowl, cream the butter, white sugar, and brown sugar together using a hand/electric mixer on medium speed until the mixture is smooth. Add the fresh raspberries and blend until the dough turns pink with speckles of raspberries intact.

Add the eggs, vanilla, salt, and baking soda to the butter mixture. Mix on medium speed until the ingredients are incorporated and smooth.

Add the flour. Mix on low speed until the flour is no longer loose, then on medium speed until the flour is fully incorporated.

Add the semisweet chocolate chips and mix until incorporated.

Line a cookie sheet with parchment paper. Using a medium-sized cookie scooper, scoop the cookie dough (approximately 2 tablespoons each) onto the cookie sheet, placing the scoops at least 2 inches apart.

Bake for 13 to 16 minutes, until the edges are browned and the tops appear fully done.

Slide the parchment paper with cookies off the cookie sheet and directly onto the counter for cooling. (If not using parchment paper, let the cookies sit for 1 minute and then remove them to cool on the counter or a wire rack.)

This recipe combines two of Leon's favorites: a chocolate cookie and crushed crème de menthe candies (Andes mints). Every December we sell our traditional Mint Chocolate Chip Cookies, a popular Flavor of the Week. This recipe is similar but punched up by using a chocolate base and adding chocolate chips to make it richer. The outcome is a cookie with the same flavor profile as Girl Scout Thin Mints but soft, gooey, and served warm.

DOUBLE CHOCOLATE MINT COOKIES

PREP TIME: 10 MINUTES

BAKE TIME: 9 TO 11 MINUTES

MAKES 2 1/2 DOZEN COOKIES

- 1 cup (2 sticks) salted butter, softened
- 1 cup granulated white sugar
- 1/2 cup firmly packed light brown sugar
- 2 large eggs
- 2 teaspoons vanilla extract
- 1 1/2 teaspoons salt
- 1/2 teaspoon baking soda
- 2 cups all-purpose flour
- 1/4 cup HERSHEYs Special Dark Dutch cocoa
- 1 cup semisweet chocolate chips
- 1 (10-ounce) package crème de menthe baking chips

Preheat the oven to 375 degrees.

In a large mixing bowl, cream the butter, white sugar, and brown sugar together using a hand/electric mixer on medium speed until the mixture is smooth.

Add the eggs, vanilla, salt, and baking soda to the butter mixture. Mix on medium speed until the ingredients are incorporated and smooth.

Add the flour and cocoa. Mix on low speed until the flour is no longer loose, then on medium speed until the flour is fully incorporated.

Add the semisweet chocolate chips and crème de menthe baking chips, and mix on low speed until incorporated fully.

Line a cookie sheet with parchment paper. Using a medium-sized cookie scooper, scoop the cookie dough (approximately 2 tablespoons each) onto the cookie sheet, placing the scoops at least 2 inches apart.

Bake for 9 to 11 minutes, until the edges are dark brown.

Slide the parchment paper with cookies off the cookie sheet and directly onto the counter for cooling. (If not using parchment paper, let the cookies sit for 1 minute and then remove them to cool on the counter or a wire rack).

Serve warm.

Note: Using standard unsweetened cocoa instead of HERSHEY'S Special Dark Dutch Cocoa will result in a lighter-colored dough with a less-rich chocolate flavor.

Warm Moment

Hello there! Last week, I ordered my girlfriend 1.5 dozen cookies with a special custom note asking her to marry me. She said yes! Thank you for offering delivery during this crazy time in the world, and for, of course, making great cookies. Maybe we can get married in a Tiff's Treats store and use the Tiff's Treats "mobile" as our weeding drive-away car? Thanks, and I hope all is well!

—Jake Palczewski

A Tiff's Treats Engagement

CHAPTER 7
WORKING WITH YOUR SPOUSE

Tiff

"How do you do it without killing each other?" That's probably the most common question we're asked when people find out we work side by side and have done so for over twenty years. We sit across from each other in a shared office. Technically face-to-face, although his monitor setup is so gargantuan that I can only see his spikey black hair peeking out from the top, and we have to stand to address each other, or we just shout into the air, like an in-person telephone call.

The short answer to that question is that we've almost killed each other many times. Working together, living together, and raising kids together is a lot of time spent with another person. Enough time where him chugging a water bottle in one swoop, instead of drinking it at a normal pace, could send you right over the edge. It's also a ton of time spent listening to him hum "Auld Lang Syne" for no particular reason, so much that you now also endlessly hum and sing it around the office. Which becomes some sort of bizarre couple's soundtrack that everyone knows you by, yet you weren't a willing participant in creating. And it's a lot of time spent with a person who has no problem telling you exactly what you're doing wrong at any given time. In no other professional setting would you hear "You are ruining this just like you ruin everything!" But in no other professional relationship would you be pushed to be better by someone who has earned the right to tell it to you straight.

And then there are the in-between times, the times we're not fantasizing about wringing each other's necks. Those are the times you're building something together—accomplishing together and failing together. It creates an unspoken bond layered with trust and respect. If the in-between times outnumber the "I can't even look at you right now" times, you're heading in the right direction. In our case, we've been doing this for so long that we don't know any different. It affords us a bliss of ignorance. We are a touch codependent and always have been.

Leon

Wow, I didn't realize how annoying I am to work with. I'll admit there have been plenty of times I've fantasized about what it must be like to not work with my wife every day. Mostly when I'm in the middle of typing an important email or letter, and she knowingly interrupts my train of thought to ask me some random question, like what I want to have for dinner five days from now. Or when we're quietly working at our desks, and she sighs or yells something like, "Ugh, dammit!" while reading something on her computer. I'll stop what I'm doing and ask her what's wrong. She'll say, "Oh nothing," and go right back to work, leaving me distracted.

People are flabbergasted when I tell them that I'm sometimes with Tiff twenty-four hours a day for the full week. This was especially the case at the beginning. After college, when we went full-time with the business, it coincided with the time when all of our college friends moved away for jobs. We were working over one hundred hours a week and probably wouldn't have had time for outside friends anyway. It did make what we were doing easier, though it's also sad that we just had each other for those first few years after college. We've never known any different when it comes to our work life, but when I stop to think about it, it does sound a bit much.

When we were younger, we were more hot-tempered, which would lead to unnecessary arguments. And being young and immature, we never separated our work grievances from our home grievances. So in the span of a few minutes, an argument about cookie pricing could spiral into an attack on each other's personalities or something even more personal. And this happened, on more than one occasion, in front of our poor staff. As we've aged, we've learned to control this more and strive to be more productive in our disagreements. But I'd be lying if I said it was easy all the time.

WHY IT WORKS FOR US

Tiff

We differ in almost every way. Leon is an optimist, a dreamer, and a persistent person who will figure out a way to get what he wants. I am a realist, practical, and a person who likes to understand exactly how something will happen rather than dream about what it will be when it's done. He's outgoing and fearless around new people, and I'm shy until I get to know you. The fact that we see the world differently means we butt heads. A lot. You'd think we would have mastered how to communicate with each other, but knowing what sets someone off and avoiding doing it are two entirely different matters.

But having different skill sets and interests means that our work divides cleanly and without argument. Leon's role is to strategically move us forward and push us to the next big thing. Mine is to make sure we have a plan to get those things off the ground. He handles all investor relations, while I manage the brand's look and feel.

If you're interested in working with your spouse, the first step is to see if your personalities and talents are complementary. If we had two of Leon, the business would have skyrocketed at first, growing fast and making waves. But it may have imploded without some structure. If we had two of me, we'd probably still have only three locations, and I'd be busy perfecting our systems before we could open our fourth.

It's also important to like each other. For all of our differences, we genuinely enjoy being around each other, and I get excited when I hear his keys jingle if he's coming into the office after me. We make each other laugh, we have fun, and somehow, we have remained best friends through it all.

If you love your spouse but prefer to spend your free time with other people just as much or more so than with your spouse, working together might not be for you. I don't mean to say that you must want to be with your spouse every minute of every day. Since our jobs differ in nature, we have plenty of meetings and appointments that we don't both attend. But I'd say we're face-to-face about 70 percent of the time. If that scares you, don't do it! No financial endeavor is worth losing your marriage and your family.

Leon

For couples who want to start and grow a business together, my biggest piece of advice is to make sure your spouse complements your weaknesses and vice versa. Our personalities are polar opposites. That causes a lot of friction personally and professionally, but that's also what makes our partnership work. The brand is much better off because we balance each other out. Because we're good at and enjoy dissimilar aspects of the business, we've never had an argument over who does what. Without any discussion, we both know who should take on a new project, based on the project's needs.

SEPARATING WORK AND HOME

Tiff

Since beginning our work partnership until the present, there has never been a divide between our working relationship and our personal relationship. They have been so intertwined that one nearly couldn't exist without the other. Many couples have rules about when you can and cannot talk about work, with certain areas or times designated for family only. This never worked for us. Creating artificial boundaries seemed stifling, so for better or worse, we let the professional and personal blend together at all times of the day.

This means that work disagreements happen at dinner, they happen in front of the kids, they happen at bedtime and sometimes in the middle of the night. But not just disagreements—we brainstorm and work through issues in these casual environments as often as we do so in the office. It's an efficient way for us to operate, but it's certainly not for everyone. We do have our kids, who keep us distracted and focused on other things, and who sometimes course correct us if we're talking about work too much during dinner. A six-year-old pointing out that you're not including everyone in the conversation is one way to realize when it's time to stop.

I don't have any advice here because I think every couple is different, and families operate in totally different ways. For my part, I don't think it's the worst thing in the world for our children to get a peek into our professional lives and have a sense that Mommy and Daddy are working together on something beyond just being their parents.

WHY YOU SHOULD DO IT

Tiff

For all the difficulties of working with your spouse, the rewards are immense. The sense of partnered accomplishment can be fulfilling. Creating something together and standing back to admire it is fun. We used to have this habit of stepping back, putting our arms around each other, and then gazing at whatever it was that was finished—a new store, a new product, a new piece of packaging. When our twins were born, we brought them home from the hospital and placed them in their cribs. Then we stepped back and put our arms around each other and looked at our newest accomplishment together.

It's incredibly neat to share so many proud moments. Not just cheering each other on from the sidelines, but being in the trenches with each other and coming out the other side victorious. And then there are the times you come out not so victorious. The times when you're failing and overwhelmed and not sure what to do next. You're going through it as a team. Rarely do you feel isolated and alone and like nobody understands. He's there. He's always been there—and you'll both get through it, together.

Leon

I wouldn't advise every couple to go into business as partners. It takes a perfect storm to succeed in any business, and throwing a relationship in the middle

Bringing home the twins

will make the process harder more often than not. The stress of trying to build a business together can destroy a relationship, if it isn't solid to begin with. And it's still going to take a lot of luck and hard work, on both the business and the relationship, to succeed.

For couples who are able to withstand the tough years and the tough fights, what you get on the other side of things is one of the most amazing connections two people can have. We've seen each other and been with each other at our lowest. We've lived through all of the hard times together, through all of the fear and the doubt. Together, we've gone through the worst of bad times and the most triumphant of good times. All of this has created the unspoken level of admiration, trust, and love that I feel toward Tiff, because I know *exactly* what she's had to do and what she's had to overcome to get to where she is today. It's on another level and difficult to explain unless you've been through it. I'm extremely grateful that we get to experience all of this together.

With these holiday-inspired goodies, we can have Christmas anytime. The first time we ran this flavor was during the summer, in celebration of Christmas in July. It takes some effort to crush the pepper-mint candies, but the result is a refreshing and light cookie with a bit of crunch and chewiness. I find these hard to stop eating, and if you like candy canes and white chocolate, this is one you'll crave no matter the season.

WHITE CHIP PEPPERMINT COOKIES

PREP TIME: 10 MINUTES

BAKE TIME: 9 TO 11 MINUTES

MAKES 2 1/2 DOZEN COOKIES

- 1 1/8 cups (2 1/4 sticks) salted butter, softened
- 1 cup granulated white sugar
- 1/2 cup firmly packed light brown sugar
- 2 large eggs
- 2 teaspoons vanilla extract
- 1 1/2 teaspoons salt
- 1/2 teaspoon baking soda
- 2 1/3 cups all-purpose flour
- 1/2 cup crushed peppermint candy
- 1 cup white baking chips

Preheat the oven to 375 degrees.

In a large mixing bowl, cream the butter, white sugar, and brown sugar together using a hand/electric mixer on medium speed until the mixture is smooth.

Add the eggs, vanilla, salt, and baking soda to the butter mixture. Mix on medium speed until the ingredients are incorporated and smooth.

Add the flour. Mix on low speed until the flour is no longer loose, then on medium speed until the flour is fully incorporated.

Place the peppermint candy (if not purchased already crushed) in a resealable bag. Using a meat tenderizer, crush the candy into small pieces.

Add the white baking chips and crushed peppermint candy pieces to the dough and mix on low speed until incorporated fully.

Line a cookie sheet with parchment paper. Using a medium-sized cookie scooper, scoop the cookie dough (approximately 2 table-spoons each) onto the cookie sheet, placing the scoops at least 2 inches apart.

Bake for 9 to 11 minutes, until the edges are browned and set.

Slide the parchment paper with cookies off the cookie sheet and directly onto the counter for cooling. (If not using parchment paper, let the cookies sit for 1 minute and then remove them to cool on the counter or a wire rack).

Serve warm.

I'm not sure that carrots belong in cake—or in any dessert, for that matter. But if we're going to allow a veggie intrusion, we may as well sweeten the deal by making it into a cookie. The result is both satisfying and visually appealing. Top with homemade cream cheese frosting for a rich, indulgent treat.

CARROT CAKE COOKIES WITH CREAM CHEESE FROSTING

PREP TIME: 30 MINUTES

BAKE TIME: 10 TO 12 MINUTES

MAKES 2 1/2 DOZEN COOKIES

CARROT CAKE COOKIES

1 cup (2 sticks) salted
    butter, softened

1 cup granulated white sugar

1/2 cup firmly packed light
    brown sugar

1 cup matchstick carrots

2 large eggs

2 teaspoons vanilla extract

1 1/2 teaspoons salt

1/2 teaspoon baking soda

1 teaspoon ground cinnamon

1/8 teaspoon ground nutmeg

2 cups all-purpose flour

1 cup quick or old-fashioned oats

3/4 cup white baking chips

1/2 cup chopped pecans

CREAM CHEESE FROSTING

2 cups powdered sugar

1/4 cup (1/2 stick) salted
    butter, softened

4 ounces cream cheese,
    softened

1 teaspoon vanilla extract

1/2 tablespoon heavy
    whipping cream

Pinch of salt

Preheat the oven to 375 degrees.

In a large mixing bowl, cream the butter, white sugar, and brown sugar together using a hand/electric mixer on medium speed until the mixture is smooth. Add the matchstick carrots and mix on medium speed.

Add the eggs, vanilla, salt, baking soda, cinnamon, and nutmeg. Mix on medium speed until the ingredients are incorporated and smooth.

Add the flour. Mix on low speed until the flour is no longer loose.

Add in the oats and mix until fully incorporated. Mix in the white baking chips and chopped pecans until distributed evenly.

Line a cookie sheet with parchment paper. Using a medium-sized cookie scooper, scoop the cookie dough (approximately 2 tablespoons each) onto the cookie sheet, placing the scoops at least 2 inches apart.

Bake for 10 to 12 minutes, until the edges are browned and set.

Slide the parchment paper with cookies off the cookie sheet and directly onto the counter for cooling. (If not using parchment paper, let the cookies sit for 1 minute and then remove them to cool on the counter or a wire rack.)

Sift the powdered sugar and set it aside.

In a medium-sized mixing bowl, cream the butter and cream cheese together using a hand/electric mixer on medium speed until the mixture is smooth. Add the sifted powdered sugar and the vanilla to the butter mixture. Mix on medium speed until the ingredients are blended and creamy. Add the heavy whipping cream to adjust consistency and salt for taste. Makes 1 1/2 cups frosting.

Spread the frosting on top of the cooled Carrot Cake Cookies and serve.

There seems to be an unspoken requirement that when fall arrives, you must offer something pumpkin-spice flavored. We start getting that request each year on October 1, when pumpkin spice season unofficially kicks off. This recipe uses pumpkin puree and spices to re-create pumpkin pie in cookie form. The outcome is a simple but delicious cookie that has a cult following. We've toyed with the idea of selling something else in November, but team members beg me not to. It's a yearly favorite for many, so the Pumpkin Spice Cookies live on.

PUMPKIN SPICE COOKIES

PREP TIME: 10 MINUTES

BAKE TIME: 9 TO 11 MINUTES

MAKES 2 1/2 DOZEN COOKIES

- 1 1/8 cups (2 1/4 sticks) salted butter, softened
- 1 cup granulated white sugar
- 1/2 cup firmly packed light brown sugar
- 2 large eggs
- 2 teaspoons vanilla extract
- 1 1/2 teaspoons salt
- 1/2 teaspoon baking soda
- 1 tablespoon pumpkin pie spice
- 3 ounces (approximately 4 1/2 tablespoons) pumpkin puree
- 2 1/3 cups all-purpose flour

Preheat the oven to 375 degrees.

In a large mixing bowl, cream the butter, white sugar, and brown sugar together using a hand/electric mixer on medium speed until the mixture is smooth.

Add the eggs, vanilla, salt, baking soda, pumpkin pie spice, and pumpkin puree to the butter mixture. Mix on medium speed until the ingredients are incorporated and smooth.

Add the flour. Mix on low speed until the flour is no longer loose, then on medium speed until the flour is fully incorporated.

Line a cookie sheet with parchment paper. Using a medium-sized cookie scooper, scoop the cookie dough (approximately 2 tablespoons each) onto the cookie sheet, placing the scoops at least 2 inches apart.

Bake for 9 to 11 minutes, until the edges are browned and set.

Slide the parchment paper with cookies off the cookie sheet and directly onto the counter for cooling. (If not using parchment paper, let the cookies sit for 1 minute and then remove them to cool on the counter or a wire rack.)

Serve warm.

Warm Moment

> ♦ Top Fan
>
> **Erin Cesla Sioco**
> The man who ended up being my husband sent them to me. It worked... we just welcomed our first child a week ago!

A Tiff's Treats delivery leads to an engagement . . . a marriage . . . and a baby!

CHAPTER 8
ADDING KIDS INTO THE MIX

GETTING PREGNANT

Tiff

I am a planner. If that hasn't come across yet, you should understand that I love planning things and controlling what comes next. One of Leon's biggest pet peeves is that I begin researching the next summer's beach trip while on the airplane home from the current trip. When it came to having kids, I decided exactly when we should add them into our lives (with a little, but not a lot, of input from Leon).

But when that perfect time finally arose (I was always on the fence about having kids, so I delayed this for some time), it was something I couldn't control. I attempted to plan out a pregnancy that didn't cross over with a maternity leave during the busy holiday or Valentine's Day seasons, which was a foolish notion, knowing now that I'd struggle through nearly two years of fertility treatments, including three attempts at IVF (in vitro fertilization), before finally getting pregnant. I felt a certain duty to try my hardest to make this happen, since the problems were all on my end. Leon had always wanted children, and I didn't want to be the reason it wasn't going to happen for him.

If you're wondering whether IVF will test your marriage, it will. It's a rough process to go through physically, emotionally, and financially. We were able to sell off a small piece of the business to pay for these treatments, which we otherwise could not have afforded. We experienced different perspectives about events and different reactions to the constant disappointments and increasingly grim outlook. I was never good at understanding that my own frustration and occasional grief might also be affecting him, and that he might be having a difficult time getting through this too.

The worst part of going through significant fertility issues is the lingering fear that you might never have biological children. If you knew going through it that it was 100 percent certain to succeed, it would be an easier road to travel. But the unknown hangs heavy on you during the whole painstaking process. It doesn't help that being in your thirties means that every person you know will get pregnant while you're trying to do the same. My sister-in-law nearly lapped me, getting pregnant with her first while we were trying and her second just months after we finally had success. I believe I counted thirteen close friends and family members who told me they were pregnant during the time we were trying to have kids.

We kept our ordeal secret because we figured we didn't need any extra pressure or unwelcome check-ins when things were going poorly. This meant we were left alone about it, but this also meant that nobody knew to be sensitive to us when announcing their news, or worse, complaining when their addition wasn't expected.

Finally, one of our rounds of IVF worked. It was the last round I was willing to do before giving up or moving on to other options. Not only did it work, but when the nurse called me with my blood test results and read me the number, I was stunned. A positive should have returned a number between 100 and 200. My number was almost 600. This meant one thing: *twins*. Sure enough, a few weeks later an ultrasound confirmed twins. My mind flashed back to all kinds of waivers I'd signed, explaining how risky it was to carry and deliver multiples, but nevertheless, we were thrilled.

Pregnancy isn't easy on anyone, especially with multiples. My legs swelled to about five times their normal size, and I was ultimately diagnosed with preeclampsia, which required us to deliver the babies early or risk me having a stroke. In the hospital, I even woke Leon up in the middle of the night and asked him to bring in a doctor to check for a blood clot, because I was sure if we waited until morning, my leg—which was completely numb and felt like it was no longer a part of my body—would be dead.

But even with all of that, I'm so grateful I had the opportunity to experience pregnancy. I came close to never having that chance, and this realization gave me an incredible sense of appreciation the whole nine months. Not everyone's fertility story ends with two healthy twins, and while it was a difficult road to get there, we're acutely aware of how lucky and blessed we are.

Leon

Watching Tiff's fertility struggles was extremely difficult for me. For so long, Tiff has been the steady one, the one who doesn't get fazed by much. I was the one stressed out about the business. Tiff always dealt with the work stress a lot better than I did, but when it came to getting pregnant, it was hard on her mentally and psychologically.

When I was growing up, things seemed harder for me than they were for others. I always had to work harder; I was never the most naturally gifted at anything. Right around the time we started the business, I had an epiphany that my life would *never* be easy. I'd struggle with anything I attempted to do. But the second part of the epiphany was that even if I struggled at first, the outcome always seemed better than I could have ever hoped for. This was a pattern in my life—playing sports, learning to play guitar, doing schoolwork—nothing came easy. But when I looked back, my hard work paid off.

I believed that us struggling to have kids was another example of this pattern in my life. I told Tiff it was the "Chen Way," that this was par for the course, and that she'd married into it. Compared to many people we knew who got pregnant easily, we'd have to struggle through

a lot. But in the end, I believed we'd be in a place where we could look back and say, "Wow, we were so lucky." I didn't realize how right I would end up being with the twins.

My whole life, I'd thought about a lot of different things, imagining what job I might have, who I might marry, how many kids I'd have, where I'd live. I never once imagined I'd be the father of twins. I call them the biggest plot twist of my life.

When we found out we were having twins, Tiff was rightfully terrified, and I was thrilled. So happy that the IVF doctor had to tell me

Tristan and Taylor join the team

immediately that having twins was risky and less safe and not something I should be so thrilled about. Nonetheless, I was happy. Tiff had been trying so hard to get pregnant, and I'd seen her experience true sadness throughout the process. I never wanted to see that again. It made me feel terrible that I could do nothing to help the situation.

The moment the doctor said "twins," I hoped and felt it would be one boy and one girl. I told Tiff, and she dismissed that right away, saying, "No, I'm certain it's going to be two boys." She surmised this because my father was one of five boys, and his two children were boys.

Almost twenty weeks later, we gave the nurses at our checkup two cards and asked them to write *boy* or *girl* on each card and seal them in separate envelopes. That night, we went downtown for a nice steak dinner and turned on our cell phones to record each other. We each opened an envelope, took the card out, and on the count of three, without looking at our own card, we held it to our forehead, so the other person could see.

The card on Tiff's forehead read, "Baby A is a *boy*." I was ecstatic but not surprised, given our conversations about this. With a big grin, I looked at Tiff, who was staring at the card on my forehead. She had this incredible look of surprise and asked me about her card: "Are you surprised?"

"No, but I'm so happy," I said, then asked her, "Are *you* surprised?"

She beamed. "Yes, I am surprised."

I instantly knew what that meant. I jumped out of our booth and yelled, "*Yes!*" My card read, "Baby B is a *girl*." We had our twins, one boy and one girl.

JUGGLING BABIES AND WORK

Tiff

"Mute your line!" displayed in the chat window on my computer. I was sitting in a separate room, dialed into the meeting. Leon was letting me know that everyone in the conference room could hear my breast pump whirring in the background as I listened, trying my best to contribute. Breastfeeding twins had become like a second job for me, taking up roughly thirty-five hours a week at the peak.

Adding babies into our lives was a huge change. We were used to working on our own schedule, starting whenever we liked and working late into the night most days. We had little to no structure or daily routine. Then boom, we had these two babies who forced us into not only a routine but a daily journaling of exactly when and how much they were eating, sleeping, pooping, you name it. Our sleep-training logs alone are mind-boggling to me now. How did we have the time? Oh yeah, we were awake twenty hours a day. In any case, we had lots of work to do at Tiff's Treats. We weren't slowing down, and we needed as much focus there as we needed at home.

Leon

The twins brought so much change into our lives, so fast. I knew becoming a parent would be hard, but I also knew that I'd find it rewarding. However, that was under the assumption that we'd only have one baby at a time. I thought having twins would be like having 1.5 babies at once. Since we were already taking care of one baby, I figured there were efficiencies in having two at the same time. How wrong I was. At first, it's like having three or four kids with all the crying and screaming and overlapping sicknesses and worries.

There are many things I wish I could go back and do over again during those early years, just because it was so frantic, and we were so tired from trying to grow a business while raising baby twins. However, looking back on it, it felt like these twins were a gift that I needed. Since the business started when I was nineteen years old, I've been obsessed with it. I'd think about the business and how to improve it 90 percent of my waking hours and sometimes while I slept. It was more than a job or a career for me. As you can imagine, having this obsession was unhealthy. It's something I've worked on and continue to work on: figuring out ways to rest and relax and not always be "on."

When the twins were born, out of necessity I was forced to focus on something other than the business. If we'd had one baby, it would have been easier for me to stay focused on the business and also being a new dad. With twins, there was nobody there to hold the baby when I had to finish work, because Tiff also had a baby and had to work. The chaos and effort of caring for the twins made me so tired that at bedtime I'd fall asleep and not even think about work.

These days, the twins are no longer babies, and we're finally seeing the benefits of having two at once. I believe that my letting go of work helped the company and its leaders grow. I put in a lot of hours, but I probably work and think about work stuff about half as much as I used to. This has led to better-quality work on my end and a genuine feeling of happiness. The twins helped me find more balance and gave me another, more important, purpose in life.

Tiff

As any parent of twins will tell you, the early years are rough. We were like zombies at work, and we were at each other's throats a lot. Without fail, after a bad night of sleep, the next day we'd launch into some huge argument. You could almost set your watch by it. We're normally put-together people, but with the addition of our little bringers-of-chaos, we started slipping.

For instance, I once sat through a three-hour meeting with a group of potential investors only to discover afterward that the front of my dress was covered in chocolate. But not chocolate—baby poop. Then there was the Las Vegas trip Leon booked with his brother-in-law.

The twins at six years old

They planned to share a hotel room, but when they arrived, Leon hadn't booked them a room, and they had to scramble to find a place to stay. On another occasion, we packed up the kids and drove to Dallas for the annual University of Texas vs. University of Oklahoma football game, only we forgot all of mine and Leon's luggage and had to turn back. Then, halfway there we also realized we hadn't brought the tickets for the game. This kind of thing kept happening to us, and we recognized that we didn't have our lives under control. But we knew that, like many challenging seasons, this was temporary. We muscled through and took it day by day.

And then things just turned around. The kids became more self-sufficient, and we suddenly had these awesome people who were fun to be around. We started to enjoy both being at work and being at home. When the twins were infants, I remember waking up on a Saturday morning, thinking, *What day is it?*, but realizing that it didn't matter. If it was a weekday, I had a day of work ahead. If it was a weekend, that meant even more work being home with the babies. But now things were different. Weekends were enjoyable, and the twins had developed a truly remarkable friendship and bond. Finally, we were reaping the rewards of having twins, proving Leon's initial excitement correct.

Balancing work and family has been a roller coaster at times, but we've been able to share our business not just with each other but with the twins as well. They frequently appear on our Instagram Stories and star in the occasional baking video with me. Folding them in to the family business has been a fun adventure, and while we look forward to them having their own careers and carving out their own paths, they'll always be a part of our family business.

LESSONS LEARNED HAVING BABIES AND A BUSINESS

Tiff

Everyone's experience raising kids is different, so I don't presume to give advice on the matter. I do my best but am by no means a supermom. But I have learned a few things along the way.

- Remember that everything is temporary! You'll eventually sleep again, even if it doesn't feel like it now. Until then, give yourself some grace and know that you're likely not your most fabulous right now, and that's okay.

- Your partner is also going through a tough time. It's hard to see beyond your own fog to recognize that you're both struggling with different things. In my case, I felt totally underwater and not at all equipped to care for infant twins. In his case, he was dealing with a massive amount of poorly timed pressure at work with demanding investors. We both felt isolated in our "failures" and could have benefitted from cutting each other some slack.

- Your baby won't miss you at first. Babies mix well with work travel because as long as they're with a loving caretaker, they don't mind when you're on the road. This doesn't last long, and your toddler's chubby face will be streaming with tears, crying, "Mommy!" as you walk out the door, which can be difficult. At this stage, we had scaled way back on our work travel, so we were only gone a handful of days a year. But on the odd occasion when we needed to be away, I learned that the kids will be fine. They almost always pop back to being happy five minutes after you're gone. Closing the door and getting in the car is the hardest part.

Taylor screaming at the door as we walk off to work

- Your baby will go through phases, and these have nothing to do with you or your parenting. Our son struggled with stranger danger so severely and for so long that we thought his reclusiveness and fear was a permanent part of his personality. But one day it stopped, and he became a happy and social toddler. Since our kids are the exact same age, we can clearly see when one is going through a difficult phase because the other one will experience it exactly six months later. They switch off, almost like clockwork, with who is more difficult to handle—luckily they rarely are at the same time. Which tells us that their temperaments ebb and flow and helps us relax, knowing the phase will pass and probably isn't happening because of something we did.

- Having loving caretakers—whether family, a babysitter, or a trusted daycare center—is helpful if you can make it happen. We wouldn't have been able to expand our business and also stay home with infants. I couldn't even make a salad without one twin or the other crying for my attention. (After they were born, it was years before I brought my grandma's mac and cheese to the company potluck, because it required eight solid minutes of stirring on the stove, and that would have been absolutely impossible.) I've always thought that the more people out there who love my children, and whom they love back, the better.
- Make deals with your partner. Things like this: "If I go to the gym early and you stay with the kids, then I'll come home after work and you can stay there late." Coordinating care can be arduous, but if you learn to work with your partner and aren't afraid to ask for the concessions you need, you'll both be better and happier.
- Remember that every child is different, every parent is different, and every situation is different. What works for you might not work for your friend or vice versa. Figure out what works for you, take the advice that makes sense in your situation, and ignore the rest, including anything I've said here that doesn't help. There's no one perfect way to be a parent.

Leon

About a year before we had kids, Tiff and I sat down and made a list detailing how we wanted to raise our kids, which we called our "parenting commandments." We wanted to write this down, so that when we were in the middle of it, we could remind ourselves how we wanted to parent—what we thought would work best for us. The list was long, but here are a few of the many "commandments":

- Figure out a way to continue to go on dates and events and vacations with and without the kids; try to have a life outside of being parents.
- Say please and thank you to each other, and treat each other with respect even in stressful times, especially in front of the child as they get older.
- Never ever change the way we treat Buster (our dog and first baby). There is room in our hearts for Buster and the baby, and remember to love him and cherish him even when busy with the baby.
- We want to raise our child to know that they are the center of *our* universe, but not the center of *the* universe.

When writing this out, we never imagined we'd have twins, which made it harder to follow through on every commandment. But it was a good exercise because it solidified how we wanted life with kids to be. We knew we wouldn't get all the goals right all of the time, and we knew things would invariably change, but we did pretty well.

Tiff

We didn't succeed at all of the commandments. And some are comical to look at now. It's impossible to understand what being a parent is like until you become one. So many of our goals were easier said than done, such as: "When new people walk into our home, we don't want them to think right away, *These people have kids*, based on the way the house is kept." Fast-forward six months, and our living room had been

Our complete family,
including Buster

converted temporarily into a playroom with all of the toys stored out in the open, visible upon entry. Plus, we had multiple high chairs in the kitchen and contraptions all over the house that we never knew would be required to keep two babies alive and happy.

Nevertheless, nothing brings me more bliss than seeing my living space nice and neat and clear of all debris, like it was pre-kids. For me, it's like an endorphin rush to see it that way. This commandment is something I strive for, but I'm aware that having a messy home is just part of being a parent, and most days I try to let it go. I know that one day I'll miss the toys and drawings and discarded clothes all over the place, and the floor getting covered wall to wall in Lego bricks within one second of arriving home.

Whether we're succeeding or failing at the kind of parents we thought we might be, having the discussion beforehand of what was important to us as we embarked on this together was a helpful tool. It has allowed us to at least make an effort to hold on to our goals, attainable or not.

We sell this longtime fan favorite every October because it's the perfect Halloween treat. The color combination is perfect for being festive at Halloween parties and easier to make than a fancy spider-shaped cookie. Besides that, they're delicious and an office favorite, including for me. Even if you don't love peanut butter, these have just enough to liven up the cookie while leaving chocolate as the star ingredient.

DOUBLE CHOCOLATE PEANUT BUTTER COOKIES

PREP TIME: 10 MINUTES

BAKE TIME: 9 TO 11 MINUTES

MAKES 2 1/2 DOZEN COOKIES

1 cup (2 sticks) salted butter, softened

1 cup granulated white sugar

1/2 cup firmly packed light brown sugar

2 large eggs

2 teaspoons vanilla extract

1 1/2 teaspoons salt

1/2 teaspoon baking soda

2 cups all-purpose flour

1/4 cup HERSHEY'S Special Dark Dutch Cocoa

1/2 cup milk chocolate chips

1 cup peanut butter candy pieces

Preheat the oven to 375 degrees.

In a large mixing bowl, cream the butter, white sugar, and brown sugar together using a hand/electric mixer on medium speed until the mixture is smooth.

Add the eggs, vanilla, salt, and baking soda to the butter mixture. Mix on medium speed until the ingredients are incorporated and smooth.

Add the flour and cocoa. Mix on low speed until the flour is no longer loose, then on medium speed until the flour is fully incorporated.

Add the milk chocolate chips and peanut butter candy pieces, and mix on low speed until incorporated fully.

Line a cookie sheet with parchment paper. Using a medium-sized cookie scooper, scoop the cookie dough (approximately 2 table-spoons each) onto the cookie sheet, placing the scoops at least 2 inches apart.

Bake for 9 to 11 minutes, until the edges are set and darker brown.

Slide the parchment paper with cookies off the cookie sheet and directly onto the counter for cooling. (If not using parchment paper, let the cookies sit for 1 minute and then remove them to cool on the counter or a wire rack.)

Serve warm.

Note: Using standard unsweetened cocoa instead of HERSHEY'S Special Dark Dutch Cocoa will result in a lighter-colored dough with a less-rich chocolate flavor.

My absolute favorite cookie on our regular menu is Oatmeal Chocolate Chip. I love the additional flavor and texture the oatmeal brings, which offsets some of the sweetness. This more grown-up version uses dark chocolate chunks and adds crushed, roasted pistachios for a salty, crunchy bite. The idea to make something with dark chocolate and pistachios came from a contest we ran, where each store submitted a pitch for a new flavor of the week. This was the winner, and we added oatmeal to it for this book, since I couldn't possibly publish recipes without including my favorite ingredient.

OATMEAL DARK CHOCOLATE PISTACHIO COOKIES

PREP TIME: 10 MINUTES

BAKE TIME: 10 TO 12 MINUTES

MAKES 2 1/2 DOZEN COOKIES

- - - - - - - - - - - - - - - - - - - -

$3/4$ cup pistachios, whole roasted

$1 1/8$ cups (2 $1/4$ sticks) salted butter, softened

1 cup granulated white sugar

$1/2$ cup firmly packed light brown sugar

2 large eggs

2 teaspoons vanilla extract

$1 1/2$ teaspoons salt

$1/2$ teaspoon baking soda

$1 7/8$ cups all-purpose flour

$1 3/4$ cups rolled oats

$1 1/2$ cups dark chocolate chips

1 tablespoon sea salt flakes, optional

Preheat the oven to 375 degrees.

Place $1/4$ cup of the whole roasted pistachios in a resealable storage bag and crush the pistachios into medium pieces. Set aside.

In a large mixing bowl, cream the butter, white sugar, and brown sugar together using a hand/electric mixer on medium speed until the mixture is smooth.

Add the eggs, vanilla, salt, and baking soda to the butter mixture. Mix on medium speed until the ingredients are incorporated and smooth.

Add the flour. Mix on low speed until the flour is no longer loose, then on medium speed until the flour is fully incorporated.

Mix in the oats until incorporated. Add the chopped pistachios, the remaining whole pistachios, and the dark chocolate chips and mix on low speed until the ingredients are incorporated evenly in the dough.

Line a cookie sheet with parchment paper. Using a medium-sized cookie scooper, scoop the cookie dough (approximately 2 tablespoons each) onto the cookie sheet, placing the scoops at least 2 inches apart.

Bake for 10 to 12 minutes, until the edges are browned and set.

Slide the parchment paper with cookies off the cookie sheet and directly onto the counter for cooling. (If not using parchment paper, let the cookies sit for 1 minute and then remove them to cool on the counter or a wire rack.)

If desired, sprinkle sea salt onto the cookies after they cool before serving.

We only ran Peanut Butter Chocolate Candy Cookies once, and that was years ago. And once Peanut Butter Chocolate Chip Cookies landed on our permanent menu, this was too similar to put on our Flavor of the Week menu. I've always been sad about that because I loved both the look and the taste of this cookie. My tip is to use M&M's Minis, because they take up less room in the dough, resulting in more uniformly shaped and sized cookies. It also gives you just a taste of chocolate in each bite instead of a mouthful of just M&M's.

PEANUT BUTTER CHOCOLATE CANDY COOKIES

PREP TIME: 15 MINUTES

BAKE TIME: 9 TO 11 MINUTES

MAKES 2 1/2 DOZEN COOKIES

. . . .

1 1/8 cups (2 1/4 sticks) salted butter, softened

1 cup granulated white sugar

1/2 cup firmly packed light brown sugar

2 large eggs

2 teaspoons vanilla extract

1 1/2 teaspoons salt

1/2 teaspoon baking soda

2 1/4 cups all-purpose flour

2 tablespoons milk

3/4 cup creamy peanut butter

1 1/3 cup mini milk chocolate candies

Preheat the oven to 375 degrees.

In a large mixing bowl, cream the butter, white sugar, and brown sugar together using a hand/electric mixer on medium speed until the mixture is smooth.

Add the eggs, vanilla, salt, and baking soda to the butter mixture. Mix on medium speed until the ingredients are incorporated and smooth.

Add the flour. Mix on low speed until the flour is no longer loose, then on medium speed until the flour is fully incorporated.

Add the milk and creamy peanut butter and mix on low speed until fully combined.

Add the milk chocolate candies and mix on low speed or by hand until distributed evenly throughout the dough.

Line a cookie sheet with parchment paper. Using a medium-sized cookie scooper, scoop the cookie dough (approximately 2 table-spoons each) onto the cookie sheet, placing the scoops at least 2 inches apart.

Use a fork and flatten the tops of the dough both horizontally and vertically to create crisscross hash marks.

Bake for 9 to 11 minutes, until the edges are browned and set.

Slide the parchment paper with cookies off the cookie sheet and directly onto the counter for cooling. (If not using parchment paper, let the cookies sit for 1 minute and then remove them to cool on the counter or a wire rack.)

Serve warm.

Warm Moment

A request came in on Tiff's Treats Instagram messages from the mom of a boy named Bailey, who was turning eleven. Bailey is autistic and had to be taken out of school to be home-schooled because he was being bullied. He doesn't have many friends for that reason, so his mom reached out asking if we could make his birthday special by sending him some goodies.

She emailed me a picture of Bailey receiving the box we sent, saying that he was over the moon happy and that her heart melted.

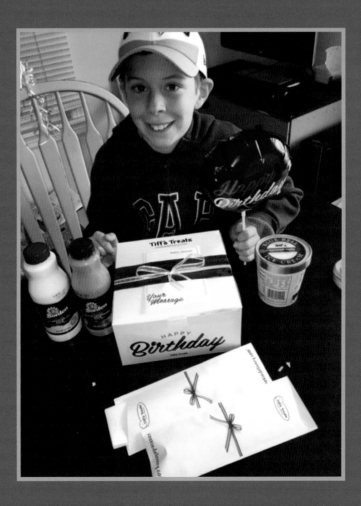

CHAPTER 9

FAMILY
BUSINESS

Leon

As I mentioned earlier, I come from an entrepreneurial family. I remember being a little boy and hearing my parents talk business ideas nonstop. I thought everybody was constantly dreaming up new businesses and talking about them. But when I met Tiff and got to know her family, I realized how unique the environment I grew up in was, at least as it related to thinking about business.

During my childhood, my mom owned myriad businesses: a retail store at the mall, a Christmas tree wholesaler, a real estate agency, and probably a few more sprinkled in between that I've since forgotten about. Early on, I witnessed what hard work and effort looked like.

Several chapters earlier, I also told you that my parents divorced when I was fairly young, and that when I was fifteen years old, they had separate businesses that took them both overseas at the same time. At first it was for a week or two, and relatives or my parents' friends would take turns staying with me. Over time their trips became longer, and eventually they both relocated overseas. Rather than uproot me to live with either one of them, I was allowed to stay behind. I learned a lot during these years and therefore was much further along in developing life skills at a younger age. While my nineteen-year-old friends were figuring out how to do their own laundry, Tiff and I had already launched the business.

Despite living by myself a lot of the time, I never felt alone. My parents didn't let me feel as though their absence was anything other than them making a living to pay for my college education. They always called and ensured I knew I was loved and that they were proud of me, even from thousands of miles away.

When I was about to start my freshman year at the University of Texas, my dad moved back to Dallas. He was and is the type of dad who would do anything I needed. At the beginning of my freshman year of college, I realized I needed my own computer. My dad had been a computer science major and was working in the telecom/IT industry, so he was knowledgeable about computers. I called him and told him I needed a computer, and he drove four hours from Dallas to my dorm in Austin to drop off the computer. I thought he'd at least stay for lunch or dinner. However, he said he had to go prepare for a busy day at work tomorrow. He drove four hours, dropped off my computer, then turned around and drove four hours back home.

From day one, both of my parents were supportive about the business. Even though I don't know if they understood or thought there'd be a market for on-demand, warm-cookie delivery, they were encouraging and proud I was trying to do something. If you'd asked them back then, I'm sure they thought the business would fail. When I was about to graduate, they approached me separately, asking about my post-graduation career or job plans. I think they both would've liked to see their son get a steady job, so they didn't have to worry about me. They'd also worked extremely hard all of their lives to put me through college. I was concerned it would seem ungrateful for me to continue with the business when there were steady jobs with real pay that my degree would have afforded me.

As you know, when the time came, Tiff and I decided to go for it. And my parents couldn't have been more supportive. My mom and my dad both took out second mortgages on their properties, so I could secure loans for the business against their houses. My mom's husband, whom she met and married when I was a teenager, was the first one to financially support us. We had needed a new oven when we were in college, and I told my mom about this. The next thing I knew, we received a $5,000 check from my stepfather. We used that to buy our first commercial-grade oven and eventually paid him back years later. What he may not have known or understood was that his belief in us—enough to loan us money on a business that could have been merely a college project—meant the world to us.

That's one thing I learned about parents and love: They didn't necessarily believe our business was a solid concept, and back then there was nothing to compare us to. Although they knew the odds were against us, they supported us and risked their own livelihoods to try to help make our dreams come true. And they did it for no other reason than love.

I'll never adequately be able to repay them for what they did; it was life-altering for us. The best I can do is to remember this love and support and find a way to help their grandchildren—my own children—realize their dreams.

Tiff

If this were a movie, this would be the point where the split screen would show what was happening at Leon's house and at my house concurrently. The environments couldn't have been more different. I don't recall a time that my family ever discussed money, jobs, business, or anything remotely in that realm. I came from an artistic family, annoyingly so, and I drew the short end of the talent stick.

While I picture Leon and his parents sitting around a dimly lit kitchen table, having a dry conversation about building wealth, my family was in front of a room full of our friends, performing a spoof of a song from *The Fiddler on the Roof*, entitled "Waffle House" (in reference to a trip we'd just taken, where there were Waffle House restaurants seemingly on every corner). We were a family that sought out restaurants with white butcher paper over the tablecloths, so you could color while you waited for your meal. We'd all work diligently to see who could create the best drawing before the food arrived.

I had a wonderful upbringing, thanks to parents who provided me with endless love, support, and laughs. I was expected to do well in school and to honor my commitments. They taught me responsibility and how to stick with things. When I was young, my mom signed me up for piano lessons, which I hated. She said I had to play for three years, and then I could quit. I quit on year three, day one. But I've always appreciated her forcing me to do what I said I would do. When I was six, I started taking ballet lessons daily, until I graduated from high school. I never cared for ballet, but I loved to dance and perform. Ballet is the foundation for all of dance, and I'm grateful to have that background, even though it wasn't always fun. It allowed me to explore other areas of dance that later became a big part of my teenage years, as I performed on dance teams and had some of the best times of my life doing it. I wouldn't have been afforded those opportunities if I hadn't spent an enormous number of hours on basic ballet technique.

So, while my mom and I never discussed business or work or what I would be when I grew up, she was instilling qualities in me that I'd later use to build my business and career.

My dad has always been my cheerleader, and I generally think he expected that I'd succeed in anything I did. He is the first to compliment me and has always provided a healthy dose of self-confidence, frequently expressing pride in something I didn't even know I should be proud of. I'm not sure if he had reservations about the business, but he supported the venture.

My mom is by far my biggest fan and would champion anything I would take on. However, she is a realist above all else, and she had her doubts about this career choice. In fairness, to most people, this business wouldn't have seemed like a wise choice straight out of college—especially to the people who'd paid your way through it. But to their credit, they allowed me to pursue it and loved and supported me along the way.

When we leased our first standalone building, my mom (a schoolteacher) put $10,000 into a CD as collateral for the lease and kept it there for nearly fifteen years. Similar to what Leon experienced, I had parents who would do anything for me, even when they didn't see the vision.

Eventually, my mom retired from teaching and came to our aid when we needed to pass off some bookkeeping work. We were too small to have checks and balances in place but too large to keep doing it all ourselves. She stepped in so we had someone to whom we could grant access to all the accounts and who we knew wouldn't run off with the money. She still works for the company in a similar capacity.

When COVID-19 hit, we were all worried about the future of the business. One of the first things she did was call me and say that if we needed to suspend her salary to help the business, we should do so. She is ready to step in and sacrifice to make sure I'm taken care of. She is one of the most selfless and generous people I know, and I'm fortunate that she's my mom.

My mom isn't the only family member who has pitched in and helped with the business. My older sister is a news producer in Dallas and was a huge help in our expansion there, even booking us a segment on her major morning news show (before being told that the conflict of interest meant it couldn't air). She connected us with a local PR agency there and continues to use her connections to help our brand expansion.

My little brother is an advertising art director by trade, and for several years, before we could afford to hire someone in-house, we used him as a graphic designer. Then, a few years back, he started his own agency, and we were their first client. He now runs all of our advertising, designing, and content creation for marketing, and we work together daily. Our photographer gets a kick out of watching us bicker during our food photography shoots, but it sure is nice to be able to easily tell the person you're working with that their idea is no good—and equally fun when they prove that you were totally wrong, and the shot looks great.

In my family, we didn't talk much about what we'd be when we grew up or focus on "career" as a pillar for happiness. I can't help but wonder: If my ten-year-old self could have looked into the future and peeked into where we are, would she be surprised? It takes me back to a video my siblings and I made for fun one year, when I was around thirteen. We recorded a baking show. I starred as the baker, my brother created the commercials, and my sister filmed and produced it. Considering that we ended up a baker, an advertiser (my brother), and a producer (my sister), perhaps it's not such a surprise after all.

THE TIFF'S TREATS FAMILY

Leon

After the first year of running deliveries out of our college apartment, we got busy enough that we needed more than one person for deliveries. When we started, Tiff and I took turns doing everything. Sometimes I'd stay back and bake the cookies while she'd deliver them, and other times I'd deliver. On more than one occasion, we were so busy that she'd be out on a delivery, and another order in the opposite direction needed to be delivered before she returned. I'd take the order and bring my cell phone, which was our company line, with me in the car. If that phone rang, I'd have to pull off the road to take the order.

After moving into our shared kitchen space with the potato shop, we decided to find some delivery drivers. We didn't know how to hire or who to hire, so we asked around our group of friends. We had come to the University of Texas with a good group of friends from our high school, and we hung out with a lot of them. Some of these friends had younger brothers, who were in their freshman year. One of them reached out when he heard we were hiring, and we had our first group of delivery drivers. Kullen, Ryan, and Scott all started the same week, and shortly after brought in another one of their friends, Michael. All four had graduated from our high school, LV Berkner High School in Richardson, Texas. They were just looking to earn some "beer money" and thought delivering cookies would be a fun way to do that. They also heard that a lot of our deliveries were to all-girls dorms and sorority houses, which I'm sure had at least something to do with their interest.

Working side by side with these "Tiff's Treats OGs," as we call them, was a special time in our lives. They worked part-time while they were in school and were an integral part of our early growth. They were with us when we had no systems and no processes, but they worked hard to make sure we provided a quality product and experience. Tiff and I were barely older than them, so they had to work for two people who had no idea how to be bosses and were figuring it out as we went along.

Some of our favorite memories from those early days include all the fun moments we had with these first employees. We're extremely proud to say that over twenty years later, all four of these "boys" are still with the company, at a director level or higher. Three out of four of them left the company after graduation, got "real" jobs, and came back years later to help us grow the brand. Michael never left and has been with Tiff's Treats for twenty years, the longest tenured member of the team outside of Tiff and me. As previously mentioned, Kullen left and got some outside experience, and he also earned an MBA and returned to be our CFO. He currently holds the title of senior executive vice president at Tiff's Treats.

In addition to the original crew, many of the college "kids" who worked for us during their undergrad years left upon graduation but found their way back. Several of the employees who worked alongside Tiff and me in those early years are with the company today, in roles like VP of finance, director of sales, and director of real estate. During those first years, we were like a family. We spent all our time at work together but also hung out with each other outside of work. Watching these kids grow up, get married, start families, and become wonderful adults has been heartwarming.

Tiff

While some people prefer to keep business and personal relationships completely separate, we have found working with trusted and talented friends fulfilling. Two of our best friends in the world, a married couple we have known since college, joined the team at different times. First in a temporary capacity, to lend a helping hand with their professional expertise, and then full-time when we realized we'd benefit from having them in permanent roles. Wendy and Brian, our senior director of HR and senior director of new projects, respectively, have been instrumental in our growth, and it's particularly fun to share the business ups and downs not only with each other but also with these two cherished friends.

Leon

It's a big risk to work with friends. It can be a spectacular success or failure, and it's not something we'd recommend for just any situation. At our wedding, my groomsmen lineup was filled with men who either worked with us at Tiff's Treats or helped along the way.

My childhood friend Matt was the only groomsman who wasn't involved in the business, but later even he joined Tiff's Treats in a director role. It has been one of the greatest joys of my life to work with these friends and share in all the successes—and even some of the failures—together.

If you like pecan pie even a little bit, these bars will knock you off your feet. The base is made from Honey Oatmeal Pecan Cookie dough (delicious on its own) and topped with pie filling and pecans for a sweet, gooey, and crunchy top. Imagine serving these bars at the Thanksgiving table, perhaps with a scoop of vanilla ice cream. You'll be invited back the next year—no doubt in charge of dessert.

PECAN PIE BARS

PREP TIME: 30 MINUTES

BAKE TIME: 32 TO 37 MINUTES

MAKES 12 BARS

HONEY OATMEAL PECAN COOKIE DOUGH

1 1/8 cups (2 1/4 sticks) salted butter, softened

1 cup granulated white sugar

1/2 cup firmly packed light brown sugar

2 large eggs

2 teaspoons vanilla extract

1 1/2 teaspoons salt

1/2 teaspoon baking soda

2 1/4 cups all-purpose flour

1 1/3 cups thick rolled oats

1/3 cup honey

1 cup pecan pieces

Cooking spray

FILLING

2 large eggs

1/2 cup light corn syrup

1/2 cup granulated white sugar

1 1/2 tablespoons salted butter, melted

3/4 teaspoon vanilla extract

1 1/2 cup chopped pecans

1/2 tablespoon cornstarch

TOPPING

1 cup chopped pecans

1/2 cup pecan halves

Preheat the oven to 350 degrees.

In a large mixing bowl, cream the butter, white sugar, and brown sugar together using a hand/electric mixer on medium speed until the mixture is smooth.

Add the eggs, vanilla, salt, and baking soda to the butter mixture. Mix on medium speed until the ingredients are incorporated and smooth.

Add the flour and oats. Mix on low speed until the flour is no longer loose, then on medium speed until the flour is fully incorporated.

Add the honey and pecan pieces and mix until incorporated fully.

Lightly coat a 9 x 13-inch baking pan with cooking spray. Place the dough in the bottom of the pan and use your hands to flatten it into an even layer.

For the filling, in another mixing bowl, add the eggs and beat to a smooth consistency. Then add the corn syrup, sugar, melted butter, vanilla, and chopped pecans and mix well using a spatula. Mix in the cornstarch then allow the filling to rest for 2 minutes.

Pour the filling on top of the cookie base layer in the pan and use a spatula to spread the mixture evenly.

For the topping, distribute the chopped pecans and pecan halves evenly on top of the filling layer.

Bake for 32 to 37 minutes, until the top is set well and the edges are browned.

Cool for 40 to 55 minutes before serving. Use a knife to cut 12 individual bar portions and serve.

One day, while I waited for my daughter to finish ballet class, I dreamed up this Peanut Butter Chocolate Bar, and that Monday, the team got to work making it a reality. The result was a peanut butter lover's dream. The most fun part about these bars is breaking one open to see its signature shiny chocolate stripe in the center. They're as fun to look at as they are to eat, although if I could do only one or the other . . . well, you know what I'd pick.

PEANUT BUTTER CHOCOLATE BARS

PREP TIME: 30 MINUTES

BAKE TIME: 35 TO 38 MINUTES

MAKES 12 BARS

PEANUT BUTTER CHOCOLATE COOKIE DOUGH

1 1/8 cups (2 1/4 sticks) salted butter, softened

1 cup granulated white sugar

1/2 cup firmly packed light brown sugar

2 large eggs

2 teaspoons vanilla extract

1 1/2 teaspoons salt

1/2 teaspoon baking soda

2 1/4 cups all-purpose flour

2 tablespoons milk

3/4 cup creamy peanut butter

2 cups semisweet chocolate chips, divided

Cooking spray

FILLING

8 (1.55-ounce) packages milk chocolate bars

TOPPING

1 cup peanut butter chips

Preheat the oven to 350 degrees.

In a large mixing bowl, cream the butter, white sugar, and brown sugar together using a hand/electric mixer on medium speed until the mixture is smooth.

Add the eggs, vanilla, salt, and baking soda to the butter mixture. Mix on medium speed until the ingredients are incorporated and smooth.

Add the flour. Mix on low speed until the flour is no longer loose, then on medium speed until the flour is fully incorporated.

Add the milk and creamy peanut butter and mix on low speed until the ingredients are incorporated fully.

Add 1 cup semisweet chocolate chips and mix on low speed until the chips are evenly distributed throughout the dough.

Lightly coat a 9 x 13-inch baking pan with cooking spray. Divide the dough into two equal parts. Set one half aside at room temperature. Place the other half in the bottom of the pan. Spread the dough evenly across the bottom of the pan and flatten it with your hands to form a base layer of cookie dough.

To make the chocolate filling, evenly place the milk chocolate bars on top of the base cookie dough layer, with no overlap.

Place the remaining half of the cookie dough on top of the chocolate bars. Press and flatten the dough with your hands until it covers the chocolate layer completely.

For the topping, mix the peanut butter chips and remaining semisweet chocolate chips together and sprinkle the chips evenly over the top layer of dough.

Bake for 35 to 38 minutes, until the top is set well and the edges are browned.

Cool for 30 to 45 minutes before serving. Use a knife to cut 12 individual bar portions and serve.

This bar is my favorite of the three featured in our signature Tiff's Trio dessert bar set. Which, of course, means it includes a lot of toffee and a lot of salt. The Salted Caramel Blondie Bar is a bit more crumbly than gooey and boasts a cookie base with caramel, caramel bits, white chips, and walnuts, and it's topped with toffee bits and sea salt. If you're taking a break from chocolate, this blondie is the perfect treat.

SALTED CARAMEL BLONDIE BARS

PREP TIME: 20 MINUTES

BAKE TIME: 25 TO 27 MINUTES

MAKES 12 BLONDIES

SALTED CARAMEL BLONDIE DOUGH

1/2 cup (1 stick) salted butter, softened

1/4 cup granulated white sugar

1 cup firmly packed light brown sugar

1 large egg

1 teaspoon vanilla extract

1 cup all-purpose flour

3/4 teaspoon salt

3/4 teaspoon baking powder

1/2 cup white baking chips

1/2 cup sea salt caramel bits

1/2 cup walnut pieces

Cooking spray

TOPPING

1 cup English toffee bits

1/2 tablespoon sea salt

Preheat the oven to 350 degrees.

In a large mixing bowl, cream the butter, white sugar, and brown sugar together using a hand/electric mixer on medium speed until the mixture is smooth.

Add the egg and vanilla to the butter mixture. Mix on medium speed until the ingredients are incorporated and smooth.

Add the flour, salt, and baking powder. Mix on low speed until the flour is no longer loose, then on medium speed until the flour is fully incorporated.

Add the white baking chips, caramel bits, and walnuts and mix until incorporated fully.

Lightly coat a 9 x 11-inch baking pan with cooking spray. Place the dough in the bottom of the pan and use your hands to flatten it into an even layer.

Bake for 20 minutes, then remove from the oven.

For topping, sprinkle the toffee bits evenly on top of the flattened baked batter so that the dough is completely covered, including the corners. Lightly press the bits into the dough to ensure they stay in place.

Place the tray back in the oven and continue baking for another 5 to 7 minutes. Remove the tray from the oven when the toffee bits start to set on top and change to a golden-brown color.

Cool for 30 to 45 minutes and sprinkle with sea salt before serving. Use a knife to cut 12 individual bar portions and serve.

Note: You may substitute a 9 x 13-inch pan if you do not have a 9 x 11-inch pan, but increase the toffee bits on the top so they completely cover the bars in a single layer. The bars will be slightly thinner with a larger pan.

These bars were aptly named because they taste like a billion dollars. Sort of like the deep-dish pizza of cookies, we took a standard chocolate chip cookie and added caramel, coconut, and condensed milk to make a thick, gooey bar that is nothing short of sinful. This one is a staff favorite and only comes around once in a while. Now you can make this version on your own while you wait for the bars to hit our menu again.

BILLION-DOLLAR BARS

PREP TIME: 30 MINUTES
BAKE TIME: 35 TO 38 MINUTES
MAKES 12 BARS

CHOCOLATE CHIP COOKIE DOUGH

1 1/8 cups (2 1/4 sticks) salted butter, softened
1 cup granulated white sugar
1/2 cup firmly packed light brown sugar
2 large eggs
2 teaspoons vanilla extract
1 1/2 teaspoons salt
1/2 teaspoon baking soda
2 1/4 cups all-purpose flour
1 (12-ounce) package semisweet chocolate chips
Cooking spray

FILLING

1/2 cup sweetened condensed milk
1/3 cup caramel sauce
1 cup coconut flakes

In a large mixing bowl, cream the butter, white sugar, and brown sugar together using a hand/electric mixer on medium speed until the mixture is smooth.

Add the eggs, vanilla, salt, and baking soda to the butter mixture. Mix on medium speed until the ingredients are incorporated and smooth.

Add the flour. Mix on low speed until the flour is no longer loose, then on medium speed until the flour is fully incorporated.

Add the semisweet chocolate chips and mix again until chips are fully incorporated.

Lightly coat a 9 x 11-inch baking pan with cooking spray. Divide the dough into two equal parts. Set one half aside at room temperature. Place the other half in the bottom of the pan. Spread the dough evenly across the bottom of the pan and flatten it with your hands to form a base layer of cookie dough.

Pour the condensed milk on top of the base layer of cookie dough, using a spatula to spread it evenly. Pour the caramel sauce on top of the condensed milk and spread/mix it evenly. Sprinkle the coconut flakes uniformly over the condensed milk and caramel.

Preheat the oven to 350 degrees, then refrigerate or freeze the pan for 30 minutes to solidify the filling on top.

Place the remaining half of the cookie dough on top of the filling layer. Press and flatten the dough with your hands until it covers the filling layer completely.

Bake for 35 to 38 minutes or until the top is set well and the edges are browned.

Cool for 30 to 45 minutes before serving. Use a knife to cut 12 individual bar portions and serve.

Warm Moment

In 2002, I was a freshman at the University of Texas. Never in a million years did I think I would meet my husband freshman year, much less meet him when ordering warm cookies to be delivered to myself.

It was a typical Friday night for kids in college. We would bar hop downtown, then head back to a fraternity house to continue the party and dance to Bon Jovi until the early hours of the morning. The details are vague (thank you, Natty Light, or some sort of concoction of trash-can punch), but I remember dancing all night with some super-cute guy and having the time of my life. When the night ended and we got home, I realized I didn't get this cute boy's last name, and he didn't ask for my phone number. I wondered if I'd ever see him again out and about.

The following morning, my girlfriends and I sat around reminiscing about the fun we'd the previous evening. Struggling to fully face the day, I did what most freshmen did back before DoorDash or Uber Eats: I called one of the only food delivery services that accepted Bevo Bucks and ordered a dozen Tiff's Treats cookies for myself—to Natalie, from Natalie. When I went down to accept my delivery, the driver was none other than Kullen Kifer, the guy I had met on the dance floor the night before. My first reaction was to shut the door in his face. (I still had makeup on from the night before). Knowing I needed to accept the cookies, I reluctantly

opened the door, took the box, and joked, "Well, now you have my number!" How unbelievably embarrassing. But somehow it worked, and I guess the rest is history.

We are now married with two kids and still living in Austin. The irony in it all is he has now gone back to work for Tiff's Treats. Kullen is the CFO of the company and brings cookies home to our children!

—Natalie and Kullen

CHAPTER 10

FUNDRAISING

THE VERY DEFINITION OF AN ANGEL INVESTOR

Leon

From 2005 to 2008, we had momentum in the business at our original location in Austin, but we were struggling to figure out how to succeed in Dallas. Up until then, we'd taken out loans if we had a big expense coming up, like building a new store. Around the year 2000, you could secure a $100,000 loan with just a signature, as banking regulations weren't anywhere near what they are today. However, when the economy collapsed in 2008, we were denied a loan for our second Austin location, which we'd already signed a lease for. Our first Austin store was only doing well enough to cover the early losses from our first Dallas store. With the signed lease for our second Austin location but no money for construction, we were in trouble. If we didn't find a quick solution, we could lose the entire business and be left with hundreds of thousands of dollars of debt.

That was when we met our first investor, Mark Melton. Mark was truly an angel. He believed in us even more than we believed in ourselves. When we first approached him, he'd never heard of Tiff's Treats, but his wife was a fan. We joke that he invested in us just to impress her.

We set up a meeting through a mutual contact and chose a local restaurant to have lunch with him. As two young kids who'd never done an investor pitch before, we didn't know what to expect. Before he showed up at the restaurant, we'd only communicated via email, so we didn't even know what he looked like. But we knew he was wealthy enough to invest in a fledgling business, and we envisioned him as a Wall Street guy in a movie, with a full suit and greased back hair. However, he was the complete opposite of that: an unassuming, quiet guy casually dressed in jeans, sneakers, and a T-shirt.

We pitched him, and he said, "I'm in. That sounds like something I'd like to do." We told him we had a store a mile away and offered to bring him there to look around, figuring that before he invested, he probably wanted to see what the operation looked like. He said, "Nope. I'm good." And then he wrote us a check for $1.2 million. The first investor pitch we ever had netted us $1.2 million!

We didn't realize that wasn't how these things usually work. Most founders struggle to raise money and face a lot of rejection, especially at the beginning. We now know how incredibly fortunate we were. It did help that we weren't raising money in year one, two, or even three. We'd been in business for nine years and bootstrapped everything before we attempted to bring on investors. That gave us time to build a brand and a track record that made it easier for us to raise money.

A year after that first meeting, in 2009, he invested an additional $1.8 million. Over the next few years, he added $3 million more. Years later, we confessed to him that he'd been our last chance and that when we met him, we'd signed a lease we had no money for.

Many companies have trouble with their investors getting overly involved in the day-to-day business. Especially investors that put in the kind of money that Mark put in. But Mark wasn't like that. He told us, "It isn't the idea I'm invested in. It's the two of you as people. I know whatever you do, you'll make it work." He was always there for us if we needed his opinion or help, but he never tried to impose his own suggestions or agenda on us. He trusted the two of us to make the right decision, even if it went against his opinion. His trust made us respect him even more and made us want to work harder to succeed, to prove that he was right about us.

As we started to scale the business, we experienced some growing pains. During one particularly stressful time period, we were sharing our frustrations at a board meeting with Mark and the other directors. After the meeting, he pulled us aside and said, "Look, I know you guys are frustrated and are thinking that you aren't doing as well as you want to be doing. I just want you to know that is because you're in it every single day and focused on so many different things at once. To me, someone who is checking in every quarter and not stuck in the day-to-day aspects of running the business, you are both doing a phenomenal job. You are making such big strides between each board meeting, and I want you to know that even though you can't see that, I can, and I'm happy with how things are going."

Those words couldn't have been spoken at a better time. We were stressed and feeling dejected because things weren't going as expected or taking twice as long as we'd hoped they would, but Mark's perspective helped us realize that things would never go exactly the way we wanted them to, and that was okay. To feel his support at that moment was a turning point for the company and for us as business owners.

Mark naturally understood something about investing that few others do. All investors want to add value—that's what they all tell you when you first meet them. And many of them do. Many investors feel that helping run the business and suggesting ideas is what's needed most. Sometimes that is helpful; oftentimes that becomes a distraction. We've found ourselves spending more time defending a position or trying to convince investors to support a plan or an initiative than we do executing our plan. Mark was always there to help us problem-solve when needed, but he recognized that the most important thing he could do for the founders and company he invested in was to encourage and support.

We try to emulate Mark with our own investments. We decide up front whether we believe in the person or the team. If we don't, we won't invest. If we do, Mark taught us to invest and be there to support and give advice when asked, but at the end of the day, to let the person or team we believe in do their thing.

Over a decade and a half later, Mark still sits on our board of directors and remains tremendously helpful. And he continues to support us and believe in us.

FORMING A BOARD OF DIRECTORS

Tiff

During our initial fundraise but before we met Mark, we told our attorney we had a nonnegotiable: we did not want to create a board of directors. This was our company, and we didn't want a group of people who weren't there every day telling us what to do. After we met Mark and he agreed to invest, he had a stipulation: he wanted to create a board and have a seat on it. We met with our attorney, reviewed the deal, and told him to write it up; we were ready to sign. He kindly reminded us that not two weeks earlier we'd firmly positioned that creating a board was a nonnegotiable for us. That's when we learned that some theoretical nonnegotiables are meaningless when you have an offer in hand.

With that nonnegotiable now negotiated, we were off to create our first board of directors. Mark was on it, and so were we. And we each got to nominate one seat. We selected Mike Joyce. Mike was a real estate broker we'd met years ago through one of our landlords. He'd helped us find and negotiate a lease on our flagship location, when our previous month-to-month lease had abruptly ended. Since then, he'd served as an advisor and mentor. Prior to getting into real estate he had owned, managed, and sold multiple food businesses. A big guy in stature and presence, Mike was loud in the best ways and wise with real-world knowledge from a lifetime in the service industry. He never hesitated to set us straight when we were making a mistake managing our team, and he once told Leon he needed to sit outside during a negotiation because he was too eager.

Mark selected Laine Pickrel. Laine was a CPA who'd been helping us with our books and had introduced us to Mark, since her husband was Mark's business partner. After a short stint doing our books, Laine had become an unofficial advisor for us. Having previously been a CFO at a company that was acquired by a publicly traded company, she saw promise in us but recognized when we were thinking too small. She pushed us to get out of the kitchen and work *on* our business instead of *in* our business. Another larger-than-life character, Laine was from the South, complete with the accent, and frequently used phrases such as "putting lipstick on a pig" and other colloquialisms so obscure and southern I can't recall them specifically but remember laughing when they'd fly out. Later on, she attended our wedding clad in head-to-toe pink, including a Kentucky Derby–style hat that couldn't be missed.

When we'd pictured a board of directors, this wasn't what we had in mind: five real people who could be honest and transparent with each other when things were going well and when they weren't. This group pushed us to grow in ways we didn't even know we needed to, like cleaning up an accounting mess in which we'd unknowingly lost $10,000 in unpaid deposits. And they told us to stop comparing employees to each other because "they hate that sh*t." Since we had no office, board meetings were held over lunch at Laine's house, in her dining room on top of her expensive poker table. Since this was our first board, we had no idea that this sense of family, openness, and support was unusual. We were lucky to be granted the freedom to work, the ability to mess up, and the not-so-subtle nudges to move in the right direction. Without the formation of this original board, we would've been years behind in our professional growth. Ultimately, we're grateful that we didn't stick to our original "nonnegotiable."

THE BASICS OF RAISING MONEY

Leon

When you accept investor dollars, you're selling them a piece of the company. How big of a piece depends on how much is raised and the valuation the investor places on the business. For example, if an investor puts in $1,000, and you and the investor agree that the business is worth

$10,000, the investor now owns 10 percent of the business. Every time there's an investment, the founders own less of the company. However, the goal is to use the funds to grow the business's overall value. The founder may own less of the business, but the hope is that it's worth more.

Let's say a founder owns 100 percent of a business worth $100,000. She can keep full ownership, but without cash, it may be hard to grow the value of the business. So she can "sell" 30 percent of the business for $30,000 cash, and she'd then own 70 percent of the business, and the investor would own 30 percent. This cash would be used to invest in the business and hopefully, after some hard work, the business's value would increase to $500,000. If that founder had retained 100 percent of the business, it would be worth only $100,000. In this scenario, she may own only 70 percent, but that 70 percent is worth $350,000. The idea here is that you'd rather own 70 percent of $500,000 than 100 percent of $100,000. In a nutshell, that's how investments work.

RAISING $100 MILLION FROM INVESTORS

Leon

When we started expanding more quickly, we needed to raise additional investor capital. However, we knew nothing about fundraising. We started off with Mark and several rounds of "friends and family" funding—not actual friends or family, but rather individuals who qualify as accredited investors, which is a way to raise funds for a smaller company. These funding rounds are usually led by an angel investor who comes in with a larger amount, and their contacts and other individuals add in smaller amounts. Mark led our first few rounds of funding, and over the years brought in several of his friends and business partners to help fund these initial rounds.

In 2014, we had expanded to Dallas and Houston and wanted to continue expanding in those markets and to other cities in Texas. We had only a handful of investors but decided to raise more capital to fund our expansion. We didn't feel ready for institutional investors, but we needed about $14 million, a sizeable chunk of cash. A few years back I'd joined the board of the Austin Chamber of Commerce, and because of my relationships there, we landed a meeting with a well-known and highly successful Austin businessman named Steve Hicks.

Steve set up a meeting at his offices, and we pitched to him and about ten of his friends. It was terrifying to be in that room, pitching to expert investors. It didn't help that the TV in the room was acting up, and we couldn't get the graphics on the presentation to look right. And it was the first time we'd encountered skepticism to our business model and growth plans. We'd only pitched to superfans (or in Mark's case, the husband of a fan) who wanted to be part of the brand and were looking for any reason *to invest*. This group knew and loved the brand, but they were disciplined investors and looking for reasons *not to invest*. Thus, we were hounded with some intense criticism of our plan. It was an eye-opening experience for us to be challenged and also not to bat 100 percent on takers for the deal. However, we knew if we could get a few of these investors on board, we could raise the entire $14 million.

Over the years, we've learned that a lot of life and business has to do with positive momentum. If you can get going in the right direction, that usually leads to a snowball effect. That theory especially holds true for raising investment dollars. Once you get the lead investor to set the terms, the momentum makes it easier to raise the rest of the capital.

Tiff

A "few of their friends" is an understatement here. While the "friends and family" round of funding was led by one large investment, the rest had to come from many smaller investments from individual family offices. This meant pitching over and over and over again, day after day, for several months. For us, pitching consisted of a roughly two-hour presentation on our business and why it's a good investment, followed by answering their questions, when they tried to prove that our business wasn't a good investment or pose ideas as to what we could be doing differently. Investors want to hear your rebuttal, so they can get more comfortable with your direction and learn more about you as a businessperson. Most investors in this category will tell you they invest in the person as much as the business—as Mark did with us—so this is a get-to-know-you time.

One guy went so far as to spend hours getting personal with us, asking us which birth-order child we were. I'm a middle child, and somehow this was apparent to him and informed his decision on whether to invest. (He didn't invest and then wanted to set another meeting later to tell us why he didn't, which we politely declined. Perhaps he was looking for a firstborn, but I guess we'll never know.)

This funding round was exhausting. We'd do pitches day in and day out, sometimes multiple times per day. And most of this fundraising overlapped with me having just had the twins, and I remember clearly hoping that some of these men would wrap it up because my boobs were about to burst. I was breastfeeding, and my need to pump was on a schedule I couldn't control. Perhaps if any women had been in the room, I could've excused myself.

During this entire fundraising round, I don't recall a single time a woman was sitting across from me. Men dominate the funding and investment space. I've always been treated with nothing but respect, but if you're raising money and you're a woman, be ready to be the only woman in the room.

After going through this process, we realized how easy we'd had it with Mark investing over $1 million at one time. We were now spending hours and hours talking with a potential investor and providing them with endless financial data to secure a $50,000 investment. And it takes a lot of those meetings to generate the $14 million we needed.

Leon

By the end of the summer, we'd raised the full amount and added several members to our board of directors, as part of the new deal. It felt great to have more stability with cash, but soon enough we needed more.

As we continued to expand, instead of needing a million here and a million there, our needs were more like $10 million or $15 million. You outgrow "friends and family" investments after a while because it's too much work to manage individual investors. Eventually, we turned to institutional investors. There's a benefit to having solid, credible partners, which is what the best institutional investors become. They impart the best practices from the larger corporations they deal with.

About a year after our round of friends and family fundraising, we received a cold call from the former VP of supply chain at Pizza Hut. He wanted to introduce us to a Dallas firm called CIC Partners, which was interested in investing. The firm was headed, in part, by Mike Rawlings, who was the former CEO of Pizza Hut and mayor of Dallas at the time. After several meetings and lots of back-and-forth between their financial teams and ours (our smart and talented CFO, Kullen, was learning by fire how to deal with sophisticated investment firms), we signed a deal with CIC Partners for an $11 million investment.

Then, in 2017, we were at it again. From time to time we take meetings with potential investors, even if we aren't actively raising money. It's a way to stay on investors' radars and form relationships we may want to have or need down the line. One of these offhand meetings was with a large and well-known financial institution. They wanted to lead an investment round for $25 million, our largest round of funding to date. This was exciting because it was validation to us that a firm like this was interested in investing that much capital. You're never sure these deals will go through. And thank God that while we were negotiating with them, we didn't know the odds.

After we closed the deal, they told us that they look at hundreds of deals each year, but only twenty-five to thirty of those make it to negotiations. And of those, only one or two get to the finish line. While we were confident we'd get a deal, we had no idea how far from closing we were.

Tiff

The $25 million deal wasn't easily won. Our initial meetings went well, and we were pleasantly surprised that the people attached were nice and approachable. I'm more wary than Leon when it comes to bringing on new people. It's not productive for me to have someone across the table who is brash and rude, since I'll likely shut down in that situation. Plus, I feel that life is too short to deal with jerks.

But as nice as they were, they had to crunch the numbers and make it work. As we approached the finish line, something gave them pause, and they decided to pull out of the deal. The frustrating part was that when we initially started discussions, we didn't need the money. They had approached us, and we had accepted. And while we didn't need the money, we had our minds set on it happening, and now it was difficult to emotionally untangle from that. Plus, Leon will never let something go. If he has his mind set on it, it's going to happen. Period.

One night, after the kids were asleep, he hashed out a new agreement. And he did so in our bedroom closet, the only place where he could talk loudly without disturbing me or the twins. He saved the deal at the last minute.

When the deal funded, Leon was in Vegas. I was sitting at the office, in a meeting with a few members of our team who didn't know about the deal. Suddenly, a text popped up from Leon: "Don't say this out loud, but there's $25 million in our account." I grinned, but I didn't say a word.

Leon

Unlike friends and family, who invest their own money, institutional investors are investing other people's money. So while they need to believe in the brand and in you as a person, they need to make money first and foremost. They can like your product and like you, but if the numbers don't work out in their favor, they won't invest. They also bring pressure and want you to hit certain milestones by certain times. That was new to us: answering to people who demanded answers.

I remembered back to the old days, when we weren't sure how we were going to make payroll and were anxious, fighting to survive. I would've thought raising $25 million would alleviate the stress of running a business. It did to some degree, but what I didn't realize is that the stress is replaced by pressure. Pressure to succeed because so much is riding on our success, and many people are counting on it. It's difficult to describe, but it's a completely different feeling than stress, neither worse nor better.

To date, we've raised close to $100 million to fund our growth. When people hear this number, they're impressed, but we always laugh about how what would be truly impressive is to be able to grow with as *few* investment dollars as possible. If you can make a business work without raising money, you own it all, both financially and operationally. However, our focus on investing in our proprietary technology and the cost of opening physical stores requires a decent amount of cash. We've always viewed the fundraising process as a necessary evil, in regard to how much time and energy it takes.

People often ask our advice on raising investment capital. With fundraising, what accelerated our momentum was when I decided years ago to leave my comfort zone and start networking in the community. After our early years of struggle, we established a nice groove before we started expanding faster. I was being asked to join the boards of directors for various organizations. Most of these were wonderful, charitable causes and important community organizations, like the Austin Chamber of Commerce.

At first it was easy to say no to these requests, but as we started becoming more known in the city and the brand was gaining traction, the requests continued coming in. I'm naturally outgoing, but I don't love organized activities. Especially when for so long, all my time, energy, and focus had been on running the business. However, as we were growing, I felt I needed to give back to the community and join some of these boards. I also knew that sitting on these boards would be a great way to meet other successful business owners.

I was on the board of the Austin Chamber when I also joined some great causes like Foster Angels of Central Texas, the Seton Fifty, and a local consumer packaged goods incubator, then known as the Incubation Station, now rebranded as SKU. Through these connections, Tiff and I met many of our investors and were opened up to being part of the community as a whole. We also found some great mentors in the process, people who have helped guide our growth. Best of all, we made some wonderful friends along the way.

One of our greatest days in business was when Mark was able to cash in enough ownership to recoup his initial investment. To repay him for his faith in us, when we needed it most, has been indescribable. It delights us to know that today, Mark's original shares are worth many, many times his initial investment.

From Mark's first dollar of investment, we've always had a special place in our hearts for our investors. This group of men and women, individuals and investment firms, believe in our brand and the mission to connect the world through warm moments. They believe enough to invest real dollars, a significant amount of money. The responsibility to be good stewards of their capital is something we take seriously—not just from a business or legal perspective, but from a personal one. To our board members past and present: Mark, Mike J., Laine, Kurt, Lew, Steve, Lee, Fouad, Lincoln, Jeff, and Mike R., we'd like to say thank you for your trust and guidance.

Red Velvet Cookie Truffles

We first launched Red Velvet Cookie Truffles as a Valentine's Day special item. After the response to our Red Velvet Cookies, we knew this flavor had more to offer beyond a standard cookie. We mixed the baked cookies with cream cheese, dipped them in a white candy shell, and topped the treat with drizzles and festive sprinkles. Our first year we underestimated the demand and had to recruit every person who worked at the headquarters office and then some to help. We all worked day and night and barely finished in time. We termed this disaster of a process "Trufflemageddon." But when February 14 hit, we debuted these bites of heaven to rave reviews, and now I'm excited to share with you how to make a similar treat at home.

RED VELVET COOKIE TRUFFLES

PREP TIME: 1 $\frac{1}{2}$ HOURS

BAKE TIME: 10 TO 12 MINUTES

MAKES 2 $\frac{1}{2}$ DOZEN TRUFFLE
   BALLS

RED VELVET COOKIES

1 $\frac{1}{8}$ cups (2 $\frac{1}{4}$ sticks) salted
   butter, softened

3 ounces cream cheese

2 tablespoons sour cream

1 cup granulated white sugar

$\frac{1}{4}$ cup plus 1 $\frac{1}{2}$ teaspoons
   firmly packed light
   brown sugar

2 large eggs

2 teaspoons vanilla extract

1 $\frac{1}{2}$ teaspoons salt

$\frac{1}{2}$ teaspoon baking soda

$\frac{1}{2}$ tablespoon red food
   coloring

1 $\frac{1}{2}$ tablespoons distilled
   white vinegar

2 $\frac{1}{3}$ cups all-purpose flour

$\frac{1}{4}$ cup HERSHEY'S Special
   Dark Dutch Cocoa

Preheat the oven to 375 degrees.

In a large mixing bowl, cream the butter, cream cheese, sour cream, white sugar, and brown sugar together using a hand/electric mixer on medium speed until the mixture is smooth.

Add the eggs, vanilla, salt, baking soda, red food coloring, and distilled white vinegar to the butter mixture. Mix on medium speed until the ingredients are incorporated and smooth.

Add the flour and cocoa. Mix on low speed until the flour is no longer loose, then on medium speed until the flour is fully incorporated.

Line a cookie sheet with parchment paper. Using a medium-sized cookie scooper, scoop the cookie dough (approximately 2 tablespoons each) onto the cookie sheet, placing the scoops at least 2 inches apart.

Bake for 10 to 12 minutes, until the edges are browned and set.

Slide the parchment paper with cookies off the cookie sheet and directly onto the counter for cooling. (If not using parchment paper, let the cookies sit for 1 minute and then remove them to cool on the counter or a wire rack.)

For additional cooling, refrigerate the cookies for 15 to 20 minutes.

TRUFFLE BALLS

2 1/2 dozen Red Velvet Cookies

3 ounces cream cheese

2 (10-ounce) packages white chocolate melting wafers

1/4 cup nonpareils

In the bowl of a food processor, process a handful of red velvet cookies at a time until all the cookies are a fine sand-like consistency.

Using a hand or stand mixer, mix the cookie crumbs on low speed for one minute, then on medium speed until smooth (about 2 minutes). Add the cream cheese and stir for 30 seconds, then mix on medium speed for 2 minutes until the mixture begins to fold and reaches a dough-like consistency.

Scoop the cookie mix using a medium-sized cookie scooper, slightly rounded. Roll into firm, round cookie balls using both hands and refrigerate for 30 minutes.

While the cookie balls are cooling in the refrigerator, melt the white chocolate wafers per the package directions and line a cookie sheet with parchment paper.

Remove the cookie balls from the refrigerator and, using a fork or stick, dip them into the melted white chocolate one by one. Gently tap off any excess. Transfer the chocolate-covered cookie balls onto the cookie sheet to set. The chocolate will take about 3 minutes to set around the cookie balls.

Fill an empty squeeze bottle with the remaining melted white chocolate. Once the chocolate on the cookie balls is set, use the bottle to drizzle chocolate in a zigzag line across the truffles.

Before the white chocolate drizzle sets, quickly sprinkle a few nonpareils on top of the truffles for decoration and serve.

Notes:
You can store the final product in an airtight container in the refrigerator for up to 3 days.

Using standard unsweetened cocoa instead of HERSHEY'S Special Dark Dutch Cocoa will result in a lighter-colored dough with a less-rich chocolate flavor.

Warm Moment

Just want to say thank you for delivering your treats to my daughter today. You see, there is a reason I chose y'all for this occasion, which remains close to my heart. In 2019, my twenty-one-year-old daughter was hospitalized with a rare form of encephalitis that attacked and damaged her brain. She was unconscious for a couple of weeks and unable to eat for several weeks. After about five weeks of this, she finally requested a simple chocolate chip cookie. I knew an ordinary Chips Ahoy! (though good) would not suffice for this occasion, so I googled and found y'all! Your cookies were the first thing she'd had in weeks, and she was in heaven. She shoved a whole cookie in her mouth and talked about it being the best thing she'd ever had! She remembers none of this; even so, I took her back to that day today! She endured so many treatments, including IVIG (intravenous immune globulin), plasmapheresis, and chemo. Thank you for unknowingly being a part of my daughter's path to recovery!

—Sheila

CHAPTER II

OUR BAKING EVOLUTION

Tiff

As a child I enjoyed baking, and it became somewhat of a hobby for me, although I was never serious about it. Leon, on the other hand, had never made a single baked good in his entire life when we started Tiff's Treats. Our baking education has been an informal one, learning from our endless string of mistakes. The baking portion of the business is more my realm than his. I'm not an expert baker by any means, but after twenty years of cookies being my world, I've learned a few tips and tricks along the way.

FROM MIXING BY HAND TO MILLIONS SOLD

As we entered Sears, I clutched the receipt in my hand, hoping for a different customer service associate. We were returning a hand mixer that had broken. And this wasn't the first time. Over two months, we'd returned four or five hand mixers to Sears, who kept accepting them back, albeit they were likely confused as to why they hadn't held up. Each night, we were mixing large-ish batches of cookie dough, over and over again, for our growing business. The mixers would perform fine for a few weeks, but the motor would invariably stop. We knew we couldn't keep this up without Sears putting out a bulletin with our photos on it, warning their associates that we were some kind of scam artists.

This brought in a new era for us, one with our first restaurant-quality mixer. We were in the commercial kitchen space we shared with the baked potato restaurant, and we had space for the machine, a twenty-quart Hobart commercial tabletop mixer. Leon and a few of the delivery drivers lifted it onto the table themselves, and by the looks on their faces, that thing was heavy. We were able to double the amount of dough we could make at one time, and the mixer never burned out! We had some challenges while transitioning to using it, and we even created a hack where we'd lift the bowl off its rails to get a better mix at the bottom. That was certainly against the user manual's regulations, but we weren't big on doing things strictly the way they were meant to be done.

We also discovered, as we would many more times, that as you increase the batch size, you also have to tweak the ingredient proportions. I couldn't tell you why, but the same recipe doesn't necessarily scale up one for one. Once we figured this out, we were on our way. And as we expanded, we bought one of these mixers for each new location.

As we grew, so did our dough-production needs. In 2011, we realized we could no longer mix dough with a countertop mixer at each location. With so many different people creating the dough, it was difficult to train staff and manage the quality. Also, expensive machine parts sometimes went missing in the busy retail bakery environment. Additionally, we were beginning to roll out what we call "Flavors of the Week," and sourcing ingredients for small runs of dough at each location was burdensome, and the results weren't uniform.

The mixers weren't the only pain point. We were using a love-to-hate/hate-to-love piece of equipment for portioning dough into ready-made doughballs. When we introduced this expensive new machine to the staff, they insisted they could easily hand scoop dough faster than this machine could produce it. In the beginning, they weren't totally wrong. A few young guys on our team had been doing this for years and were quick and nimble at dough scooping. And the portioning machine (which we called the "Ball Machine") was sort of an *I Love Lucy* candy episode–style conveyor belt system that spit out two doughballs at a time. The machine's process was arduous, but with the exception of a few star employee dough scoopers, it was much faster than hand scooping (and easier on the wrist). Most importantly, it allowed us to get cookies in the oven faster since the dough was already portioned. This is a helpful distinction when you're baking to order on demand.

Why did we hate this thing? To start with, it was expensive. Each machine cost $16,000, and we needed one for every store. The machine also caused issues with the consistency of the look of the dough, and thus the cookies. And the waste was a big problem. We were throwing away around twenty dozen cookies' worth of dough daily at our Dallas location alone. The Ball Machine had to go.

We decided to consolidate our dough-making efforts into one large production facility, located in Austin. Our logistics partners (our ingredient supplier) would pick up the dough from the facility and transport it to our locations. We thought of this facility as a space to increase our batch sizes and designed something that looked a lot like our retail stores' kitchens, but with bigger equipment. We bought 40-quart mixers (then 80-quart mixers and later 120-quart ones). But we had no idea what we were doing. We'd never built a production space, so everything we designed and built was wrong. From too many walls and separate rooms to too few windows for daylight to shine in, to the wrong size equipment.

For instance, we installed a walk-in refrigerator similar to what we had at many of our retail locations. On our first day, the delivery person arrived to review the shipment plan and asked how he'd get his pallet lift inside the person-size cooler door. So before making even one batch, we had to replace the cooler door with a pallet-size door, appropriate for transporting large amounts of dough. As you might expect, walk-in cooler doors are not cheap.

Eventually, we purchased a full-size dough portioning machine that took up nearly the whole room. While it cost upward of $60,000, it was a better value than buying countertop machines for each new location. Plus, it spit out hundreds of doughballs in the same time the small machine did ten. Our cookies looked better too, lighter and more golden.

Funny enough, while this was a clear-cut win, most of our employees didn't care for the "new" look, because they were used to the darker dough from the previous machine. That's an interesting thing about people and change: even change that is categorically better takes people time to adjust and come around to.

Another mistake we made when scaling up related to the team. When we created this new facility, we gathered all of our dough-making staff and rerouted them to work at this facility instead of inside the retail locations. We put our best dough maker in charge as the manager. However, working in a production facility and working in a retail bakery are different. The social people we had doing light labor at the retail store, spending time in the bustling bakery with customers coming in and out and lots of team members to chat with, were unhappy at the production facility. This was much harder labor and didn't come with the upbeat atmosphere of a store. Not to mention that there were no windows, thanks to my poor planning and lack of foresight into what people need for a happy working environment. And the manager who had been so good at making dough was just that: a talented dough maker with no management experience. He was way out of his depth, and we shouldn't have put him in that position. A year later, most of the original team at the production facility had left and we started fresh with people who were looking for a job in manufacturing, not in retail baking.

Since we built that space in 2011, we've grown in size and location count by more than tenfold, which means that our dough-production needs are ever-evolving. We now have multiple dough-production facilities, and we also make brownies, bars, ice cream treats, frostings, and other fun limited-time treats. We even make and sell frozen cookie dough, which we ship nationwide. We have sold over 200 million cookies since we started, and everything we know about dough production we learned on the fly, by messing up first and fixing it later.

BAKING FAILS

The grand opening for our second Austin location (our third overall) was busier than we ever could have imagined. This was the first time we'd hosted such an event, and we hadn't known what to expect. The customers turned out early, with the first in line hours before opening. Soon after, more and more lined up, and before we knew it, we had a line wrapped around the building. We churned out cookies at a superhuman rate and sold over 1,800 dozen cookies from 9:00 a.m. to 5:00 p.m. that day.

Sure enough, smack dab in the middle of the day, disaster struck. One of the batches coming down the line was bad. How did we know it? At first, we felt a cold chill running down our spine and the hair on the back of our neck standing up. The sixth sense you experience when you're looking at a baked chocolate chip cookie, and you know something's not right.

The baking soda.

It was missing. And it was missing from a bunch of cookies that were about to come out of the oven.

The line had grown so long that customers were already waiting four hours to get their boxes of freshly baked chocolate chip cookies. And hundreds more cookies were about to be trashed. But there was nothing to be done. We threw away the offending dough and started baking again from a new batch of dough, which completely halted the customer line until the new cookies were ready.

I am certain that I cried. We've had plenty of baking fails over the years, but this one takes the cake for the worst-timed.

TRACKING DOWN THE SOURCE

We learned quickly that we needed to track the dough, in case a bad batch came out of the oven. Dough would be scooped from the mixer bowl into several airtight containers. Then, we'd label the batches with the maker's name, the date, and a unique name for that batch, to tie each container to its lot. This came in handy since we had more than our share of bad batches come through. This way you could find all the containers from that batch and easily toss them. However, I'll never forget when one crafty employee must have realized that she made a mistake mixing the dough and swapped labels with another batch. Which just so happened to be mine, and just so happened to be a batch I had already test run through the oven to make sure it was correct. When we went to toss out all coordinating containers, we found my labels on them, with the ink smeared from having been swapped.

And that wasn't the only time we had a snafu with our labeling system. Remember that each batch had a unique name, but we didn't have any naming guidelines. In the making of thousands of batches, we'd seen every name in the book. One day, someone named their batch "I quit." We aren't sure if the label was made by someone who wanted to (or did) quit their job or someone who was merely expressing being tired at the end of the day. Regardless, the "I quit" masking tape label dislodged from the top of the container and fell into the dough.

You can imagine our surprise when a customer called to inform us that her delivery arrived with a hidden message in one of the cookies: the tape proclaiming "I quit." Not exactly the warm moment the customer was hoping for, but she was a good sport about it. I think she was more concerned about us having a saboteur employee than she was about her ruined cookies. (Of course, we delivered a new batch to her.) After that incident, we phased out the use of labeling tape and the free-form naming process!

HOW TO AVOID YOUR OWN FAILS

If I've learned anything, it's that you should be prepared for a baking fail to happen here and there, because frankly it's hard to avoid. While it's impossible to sidestep all mess-ups, I've put together a few of the top reasons your cookies may not come out the way you were hoping. I'm reminded of a time that a friend texted me a photo of her finished "cookies," which was simply a flat sheet of continuous shiny, sticky glaze with a note saying she would stick with Tiff's

Treats from now on after forgetting the eggs altogether. Eggs are kind of a biggie, but even small mistakes can end with inedible cookies, so here are a few secrets I've compiled on some easily avoidable oopsies.

MEASURING IS BORING BUT ESSENTIAL

Something you should know about baking is that it's not terribly forgiving. Every measurement should be carefully performed. When hiring people to make the dough, we generally passed over those who had a culinary interest in favor of those who had no experience but were detail-oriented. We got a lot of applicants who were excited to experiment and get creative with the dough. For customers, consistency is key, so there was no room for creativity when making batches. Each batch needed to be exactly the same as the last, to produce a cookie quality our customers could rely on.

WHY AREN'T MY COOKIES BROWNING?

In the case of the missing baking soda, we knew right away because the cookies had a dry look and didn't become the golden color that usually develops after the proper amount of time in the oven. They also had a slight lemon smell. Once you get used to those slight variations, you know it when you see it. We consider these "bad batches" to be more like scones than cookies. And God love 'em, we do not sell scones.

THE BIG THREE

In our first few years of business, I trained all of the dough makers. One tip I always shared in the training was to be aware of the "Big Three," as I called them: salt, baking soda, and vanilla. While all ingredients in the batch are critical and must be measured properly, the Big Three are especially important because they're easy to leave out or double up. If your mind wanders, it's difficult to remember if you've added these ingredients, and when you look into the mixer bowl, it's impossible to tell whether they're in there. They're used in such small quantities, and it doesn't help that baking soda, salt, sugar, and flour are all white and look similar. Mismeasurement of any of the Big Three results in certain ruin.

WHY ARE MY COOKIES FLAT/FAT?

And then there's the flour. I can't tell you how many times we've made batches with tiny, tall, and dry cookies. And equally how many times we've had flat, gooey, pancake-looking cookies. You use so much flour in a batch of cookies that measuring out the right amount is tedious but crucial. The wrong flour amount is probably the single most frequent cause of an imperfect batch.

One struggle we faced was what we called the "bottom of the batch." The dough from the last quarter of the batch always baked out flat. We realized that the paddle in our stand-up mixers wasn't getting the flour all the way to the bottom of the bowl, resulting in dough that didn't have the proper amount of flour mixed in. We came up with a solution: scoop out the top three-fourths of the batch into its containers, splash what was left with a bit more flour, and mix again. An easier solution for home baking is to make sure your mixer goes all the way to the bottom and sides of the bowl, fully incorporating your ingredients. You'll face similar problems if you have a glob of butter or brown sugar that doesn't get broken up. You'll see that ugly fella when he comes out of the oven, and you'll be one cookie down. Which, by the way, happens to me even now.

A few years back, a local magazine ran a story on us, and the writer wanted to come to our house and bake with us while we talked. The batch came out great except for one gnarly dude that was flat and greasy. Of course, the writer snapped a photo of the whole tray, with twenty-three beautiful cookies and one hideous little monster. Which is exactly why you shouldn't be conducting an interview while mixing cookie dough.

WHY IS THE DOUGH GETTING OILY?

While all ingredients must be well incorporated, you also want to avoid overmixing the dough. Mixing for too long can cause the cookies to come out flat and the dough to get dark and oily.

153

I remember once walking into a store where a team member was talking while the mixer was running. And running and running and running. I almost leapt across the room to turn the mixer off. Yes, it's important to incorporate all the ingredients evenly so that the batch is perfectly smooth, but then stop the mixer! Or, if you're doing a smaller batch and feeling up to it, you can mix by hand. That was my original method, until I realized how much easier a mixer was on the arm.

KNOWING YOUR OVEN

Making the dough is the more time-consuming part of the cookie-making process, but baking the dough is equally important. Getting the temperature and baking time right are critical for success. But here's the most challenging part: All ovens are different. I mean *really* different. You may have to have some get-to-know-you time with your oven before you feel confident about the baking temperature and duration. A good starting point is 375 degrees for ten minutes. But depending on your oven, it could be as low as 300 degrees, or you might have more success at 350. Your cookies might be done baking at nine minutes, but it might take fifteen. It's always a good idea to start low on the time, check on them, and add an extra minute if needed. One tip for when to take them out: You should feel slightly concerned that they aren't done, because the tops are light. That's when to get those suckers out of there. I can't tell you how many times I've second-guessed if they were done and given them a bonus minute, only to be disappointed by the resulting dry, crunchy cookies.

People's taste in cookies varies about the same amount as ovens do. Some people prefer more browned, crisper cookies. Others prefer them soft and gooey. I'm in the latter group—the type of person who would bake cookies for eight minutes and then eat the hot, gooey pile with a fork. That's extreme, so for our brand we lean toward the soft and gooey, but we bake them all the way through.

When it comes to baking time, there are no shortcuts. Believe me—we've tried. As you may recall, we started out in Leon's rented college apartment, which was built around 1981. It had an old electric oven, and we did the best we could with it. When we finally moved to the shared kitchen space with the baked potato restaurant, we used the money we'd made to buy a double stack of used residential ovens, which were likely from the early '90s.

About a year or two in, Leon's stepfather announced that he'd loan us $5,000 for the business. We knew what we wanted: a commercial convection oven. You see, we'd heard that while a home oven took fifteen minutes to bake a set of cookies, a commercial oven would only take five minutes. Our whole business model was based on baking to order and delivering still-warm cookies. If we could shave ten minutes off the baking process, we could potentially handle way more business and halve delivery times.

So we ordered the oven and had it installed. We cranked up the temperature to 375 degrees and baked the cookies for five minutes. It worked! The cookies were done; we boxed them up and sent them on their way. About a minute after the delivery was made, the customer called. The cookies weren't baked through. At all. The outsides were browned and appeared to be done, but the insides were completely raw.

We found out the hard way that with a commercial oven, we needed to turn the temperature way back down and bake the cookies for the full fifteen minutes. There was no magic oven that could do the impossible. We have spent over twenty years looking for just that kind of oven, just that kind of temperature, just that perfect setting. It doesn't exist.

In the end, we weren't able to shave any time off of our baking process, but we have always agreed that getting the product right, and fresh from the oven, is worth a bit of extra time. We have leaned into it and realized that our "slow bake" process—baking the cookies on a low temperature for a longer amount of time—is the secret to our perfectly baked, soft, gooey cookies.

BUYING THE RIGHT SUPPLIES

Another key to cookie baking is the baking sheet and baking supplies. Buying a five-dollar cookie-dough scoop means your cookies all come out roughly the same size and roughly in the shape of a circle (which is the goal!). For the whole first year of our business, we used a spoon to eyeball the right amount of dough onto the sheet in whatever shape it wanted to be. We have to hand it to those original customers for continuing to come back for more. The cookies must have been tasty, because they sure weren't pretty. I remember well the first day we bought a scoop. It was like we had just discovered fire. Game changer!

The right cookie sheet is helpful too. Home ovens tend not to circulate heat well. Therefore, you need to watch the bottoms of your cookies because they'll brown faster than the tops. A hallmark sign of a cookie baked at home versus at a bakery is a brown bottom. I get frustrated when I burn the bottoms of my cookies at home. Why didn't I take them out sooner? Because

I could see the tops, not the bottoms. So again, take them out when you think they aren't quite ready. The bottoms probably are. And there's an easy way to help with this issue: use an insulated cookie pan. It has a pocket of air on the bottom that prevents the heat from getting so close to the underside of the cookies.

One final, easy-to-do tip: use parchment paper. A roll of parchment paper is sold at most grocery stores in the baking aisle. I'm not sure when we stumbled upon this, but I don't remember ever baking for the company without it. Line the cookie sheet with parchment paper, which helps with overcooking but more importantly allows you to slide your cookies right off the cookie sheet to cool on the counter. With no mess! Once you're done, you can toss the paper and wipe down your tray, which will be almost perfectly clean.

DANGLERS

Spacing is important when baking cookies. If your dough is too close to the edge of the tray, it will ooze over the side while baking. We call these "danglers." And danglers don't just result in an oddly shaped half-cookie; they also drip onto the rack below them and ruin an innocent doughball minding its own business. Or they drip to the bottom of the oven and create a distinct I'm-about-to-set-the-house-on-fire smell.

If you space the cookies too close together, they'll smash into one another and create monster cookies that aren't round and aren't baked around the edges. When in doubt, give them extra space. But if your oven has a fan, and you're using parchment paper, get those doughballs in the sweet spot: close enough to the edge to hold down the paper but not so close as to fall overboard. If the doughballs aren't weighing down the paper, the fan will blow the paper upward and create an unsightly ridge on the side of your cookie. It's an art, not a science, and practicing with your own oven is the way to master it.

FAILING IS NORMAL

Every time you bake it's an adventure, and even though I've been doing it for many years, I'm still nervous about nearly every tray I bake at home. So many things can go wrong, and a lot of on-the-spot judgment must be used. I probably fail as much as I succeed. But the great thing about cookies is that they're fairly simple and quick to make. And unlike a cake or pie, where you have *no* idea what's going on inside it, you have a clear view to the product as it bakes. Also, you don't have to be an expert baker to make great cookies. I bake with my kids for fun and usually choose to make cookies because even for six-year-olds, they're quick and easy. No matter whether you fall into the "crispy" or "gooey" group, most cookies made from scratch will be delicious. Even the ugly ones.

Though we can't put toppings on our warm, delivered cookies because of the melted mess they'd become en route, at home I can play with all kinds of combinations. This is a fun way to incorporate a chocolatey hazelnut spread with your cookies. Topped with a fresh strawberry and crunchy hazelnuts, it's almost like eating a chocolate-covered strawberry on top of a cookie. This recipe is rich and delicious but simple to make.

HAZELNUT STRAWBERRY THUMBPRINT COOKIES

PREP TIME: 15 MINUTES

BAKE TIME: 9 TO 11 MINUTES

MAKES 3 DOZEN COOKIES

COOKIE DOUGH

1 1/8 cups (2 1/4 sticks) salted butter, softened

1 cup granulated white sugar

1/2 cup firmly packed light brown sugar

2 large eggs

2 teaspoons vanilla extract

1 1/2 teaspoons salt

1/2 teaspoon baking soda

2 1/4 cups all-purpose flour

TOPPING

3/4 cup hazelnut spread

1/4 cup chopped hazelnuts

10 fresh strawberries

Preheat the oven to 375 degrees.

In a large mixing bowl, cream the butter, white sugar, and brown sugar together using a hand/electric mixer on medium speed until the mixture is smooth.

Add the eggs, vanilla, salt, and baking soda to the butter mixture. Mix on medium speed until the ingredients are incorporated and smooth.

Add the flour. Mix on low speed until the flour is no longer loose, then on medium speed until the flour is fully incorporated.

Line a cookie sheet with parchment paper. Using a medium-sized cookie scooper packed flat (not rounded), scoop the cookie dough onto the cookie sheet, placing the scoops at least 2 inches apart.

Bake for 9 to 11 minutes, until the edges are browned and set.

Slide the parchment paper with cookies off the cookie sheet and directly onto the counter for cooling. (If not using parchment paper, let the cookies remain on the tray.)

Immediately press the back of a teaspoon into each cookie to create an indention about 1 1/2 inches wide.

Allow the cookies to cool, about 20 minutes.

Spoon 1 teaspoon of hazelnut spread into each cookie indention, using a knife to remove it from the spoon and spread it onto the cookie. Top each cookie with 1/4 teaspoon chopped hazelnuts.

Slice the strawberries into quarters and top each cookie with a fresh strawberry slice before serving.

Once you have a good base recipe, you can do a lot of fun things with cookie dough. This one takes our classic Chocolate Chip recipe and turns the cookies into tiny cups, ready to be filled with anything you want. In this recipe, I've filled them with caramel, pecans, and sea salt to make a cookie version of a Turtle. Cute and bite-sized, these pack a chewy and crunchy burst of flavor.

CHOCOLATE CHIP TURTLE COOKIE CUPS

PREP TIME: 1 1/2 HOURS
BAKE TIME: 8 TO 10 MINUTES
MAKES 4 DOZEN COOKIE CUPS

COOKIE DOUGH

1 1/8 cups (2 1/4 sticks) salted
   butter, softened
1 cup granulated white
   sugar
1/2 cup firmly packed light
   brown sugar
2 large eggs
2 teaspoons vanilla extract
1 1/2 teaspoons salt
1/2 teaspoon baking soda
2 1/4 cups all-purpose flour
1 (12-ounce) package
   semisweet chocolate
   chips

FILLING

1 1/2 cups caramel bits
4 tablespoons heavy
   whipping cream
3/4 cup pecan halves
Sea salt

Preheat the oven to 375 degrees.

In a large mixing bowl, cream the butter, white sugar, and brown sugar together using a hand/electric mixer on medium speed until the mixture is smooth.

Add the eggs, vanilla, salt, and baking soda to the butter mixture. Mix on medium speed until the ingredients are incorporated and smooth.

Add the flour. Mix on low speed until the flour is no longer loose, then on medium speed until the flour is fully incorporated.

Add the chocolate chips and mix again until the chips are fully incorporated.

Scoop 1 tablespoon of dough into each section of an ungreased mini muffin tray.

Bake for 8 to 10 minutes, until the edges are browned and set.

After taking the tray out of the oven, immediately press the back of a teaspoon into each cookie to create an indention about 1 1/2 inches wide. If the indention fills back in, try pressing with the end of a wooden spoon to re-create it. Let the cookie cups cool for at least 30 minutes in the tray. Pop out each cookie cup and place them on a flat surface.

In a small pot over medium/low heat, melt the caramels with the heavy whipping cream until smooth, stirring constantly. Pour the caramel sauce into each cookie cup until it is even with the top.

Press one pecan half into each caramel center while the caramel is still warm.

Top the cookie cups with a sprinkle of sea salt.

Warm Moment

I just wanted you to know how much someone's thoughtful gift meant to my family. We don't know who sent it. Our dog just passed away....

So, this just got delivered yesterday... and it's so sweet. Not sure who helped Max send it but it's making me laugh and cry all at the same time....just like Max to order cookies. Once a cookie thief always a cookie thief.... 😊 🐾

Hey guys! It's wonderful here! There's bones and balls, and Lucy! I love you and miss you, but try not to be too sad. Thank you for being a great family. Have a Merry Christmas!

- Love, Max

A furry family member gives
a final gift to his humans

CHAPTER 12

RECIPE FOR SUCCESS

Leon

From time to time we get invited to speak at events or keynote a conference or meeting. These are sometimes at universities for students or at conferences like the annual South by Southwest (SXSW) conference in Austin. We've done speaking engagements at corporate events for Southwest Airlines, Dell Technologies, and many others. Some of the questions we're most asked are about how we can stand working with our spouse, what our favorite cookies are, and what our advice is for aspiring entrepreneurs. For us, it's always somewhat uncomfortable to dole out advice, because each business and each situation is unique. While we can't say we know what will work for everybody, a few things have seemed to work for us.

SAY YES, THEN FIGURE IT OUT

Leon

When we started out, we had no plan, much less a formal business plan. If we'd taken the time to scope out the project and weigh the pros and cons of starting a business concept that had never been done before—while we were sophomores in college—there's no way we would have chosen to give it a go.

When the University of Texas called to order those seventy-five dozen cookies, along with punch, for seven weeks in a row—we'd never done that type of order. We said yes immediately, not even thinking through what an order that size would mean. If we'd told them we had to think about it, they could have, and likely would have, found another vendor to handle their order.

When we were asked to leave our location in the Scientology building and then opened our flagship Austin location, we signed the lease, remodeled the space, and moved in because that was what we had to do. If we'd stopped to calculate the odds of successfully doing that, it would have been less than 1 percent. We would have seen that we probably had less than six months' worth of cash left in the bank to sustain the business. On paper, it wouldn't have made sense to continue.

If we hadn't said yes to certain things, then figured them out later about one hundred different times, we wouldn't be in business today. These days, we're a lot more careful and measured in our decision-making process, but we continually remind ourselves and our team not to overanalyze every situation. If you know what you need to do, be confident that you'll figure out the "how," and say yes.

LAUNCH FIRST, PERFECT LATER

Leon

The number one mistake I see new founders and experienced leaders make is to try to perfect something *too much* before launching. Many times, you have no idea what you need until you put it out there. A good example of this is when we built the software for our company. If we had tried to build what we thought was the "perfect" system, it would have taken us forever. By the time we launched it, it would have already been outdated and needed to be redone immediately. Instead, we built a system that did the basics of what we needed, and over the years let the system evolve by adding features as our company has grown. During this process, we discovered that many things we thought we needed, or thought were most important, were soon replaced by new issues, problems, and opportunities. We would have wasted precious resources, time, and money, specifically, if we'd tried to build version 4.0 before launching version 1.0. One of the most underrated but learnable skills is how to iterate.

FIND A NICHE AND STICK TO IT

Tiff

Hands down, the most frequent response we receive when delivering a box of cookies is: "They're still warm!" Well, of course they are—that's what we do. From the start, we decided that delivering our cookies not only warm, but also right out of the oven, would be our niche. This means that the cookies aren't baked in advance. Right before your order is due, the cookies are put on a tray and popped in the oven. Once they come out of the oven, we have a short window to allow the minimum cooling time for the cookies to keep their shape, before they're packaged into a box, just for you, while still hot. If we miss that window and let the cookies cool too long, we have to start over again and bake a fresh set of cookies.

It's not always easy to stick by your convictions, especially when operating another way could shave off money and time spent in the kitchen. It would certainly be easier and faster to bake bunches of cookies, shove them all under a heat warmer or in a heat box, and then box up the still-warm-but-not-as-fresh cookies when an order comes in. To us, that would be like a customer ordering from a pizza restaurant, but instead of baking a fresh pizza for the delivery, the staff grabs slices from their pizza buffet station and delivers those.

We believe in the quality and the magic of "fresh baked." Any order placed in advance isn't made until right before it's delivered or picked up. We built our business on the idea that getting right-from-the-oven cookies was something special, and for as many times as we have adapted and grown over the years, one thing we've never compromised on is baking cookies to order. We are steadfast in this process, which has remained roughly the same throughout our twenty-plus years.

TRUST YOUR GUT

Leon

When facing a tough decision, one that can go either way, use your gut as the tiebreaker. We've learned this the hard way repeatedly, but the most memorable time was years ago, when I did my last hire at one of the stores. We had three locations, and someone interviewed and hired our store staff for us. For the first many years, Tiff and I had hired everybody, so when our hiring person was unavailable one day, I stepped in to conduct an interview, even though my skills were rusty. We had a guy—let's call him David—come in for an interview to be a delivery driver. I spoke to him for about fifteen minutes. It was a normal interview, but throughout it, something about him didn't sit right with me.

I went home that night, and Tiff asked me how it went. I told her, "He said all the right things, answered all the questions, but something about him makes me think he wouldn't be right for us. There was something about him that I can't put my finger on. I'm torn about whether or not we should hire him."

Tiff replied, "Well, it doesn't sound like you're saying anything indicating that we shouldn't hire him." I tried to articulate my thoughts and feelings, but I couldn't. So I hired David.

On David's first day of work at the store, I was on my way to check in when the manager of the store called me and said, "Uh, Leon . . . I don't know about this guy. Can you get up here quick?"

When I arrived at the store, everyone was standing around uncomfortably, and David was in the kitchen. He was wearing the standard-issue Tiff's Treats polo, but he also had a giant red sweatshirt draped over his head, with a hat on top of the shirt. During those early days, we issued a nice polo shirt to new delivery drivers, but we required them to bring their own hat to wear, to adhere to the local health department ordinance for food service establishments.

The manager, Jace, pulled me aside and said, "So this guy David was already forty-five minutes late on his first shift and comes in without a hat, which we told him he needed to have. We had some spare hats here, so I offered to let him wear one of those, but he refuses to wear it because he doesn't want someone else's hat touching his hair. He said he would wear his bright red sweatshirt on his head and then put the hat on top of it, so the hat wouldn't touch him. On top of that, he's already argued with me about that and some other stuff, while I'm trying to get him trained. I just don't know about this guy, man."

I told Jace that David needed to have a hat worn properly on his head; it wasn't something we could let slide. Jace sheepishly went over and asked David to wear the hat on his head. He argued with Jace some more, then walked out to his car to look for his own hat. I looked at Jace, who is normally a go-with-the-flow guy, and saw dread in his eyes. I regretted that I'd gone against my gut and hired David, who was causing so much trouble on his first day. I told Jace, "Okay, I hired this guy. I'm going to fire him for you." A look of relief swept over his face.

I walked outside to find David to fire him. He was outside his car but leaning into it through the open door, digging around the back seat for his missing hat. As I approached him, I saw the entire store staff peeking out the window, watching what would happen next. It was awkward because he'd just started work a few minutes ago, and I was about to fire him.

"Hey, David, I'm sorry—it's just not working out. You're already forty-five minutes late on your first day, arguing with your boss, refusing to do things. I'm going to have to let you go," I said.

David turned around with an angry look on his face. I don't know why I did this, but those staff polos were expensive, and he'd only been wearing his for a few minutes. I said, "And I'd like that polo back."

David's face turned bright red and even angrier, and he took off his shirt right then and there. Standing bare-chested in the middle of the parking lot, he crumpled up the shirt. While he threw it back to me, he said the weirdest line any person has spoken to me before or since:

"Don't mess with a f***ing *god*. You just might find yourself in hell."

I caught the shirt, and my mouth opened to respond to him, but I didn't know how to respond to that. So I just stood there with my mouth open. He jumped in his car and sped away.

Luckily, David never came back, and we never heard from him again. But the whole ordeal was strange and legitimately scary. I called the police to ask them to patrol near the store for the next few hours, much to the staff's relief. That day, I gave up my delivery driver hiring duties, and we all learned a valuable lesson in trusting your gut. From that moment on, for any decision big or small, I go with my gut—no matter what anybody else says or what any analysis shows.

LEARN FROM YOUR FAILURES

Tiff

In our history, we've possibly had as many failures as successes. At the end of each year, we create "Top Ten" and "Not Top Ten" lists of the ten best and ten worst things we did that year. Besides getting a cathartic laugh out of the worst things list, it gives us a chance to reflect and see what we can learn from some of the more spectacular failures. One failure that comes to mind we lovingly call "salt in the sugar shaker."

It was Valentine's Day, around 2007. The day got off to a great start. We were swimming in business but handling it well. A news crew even stopped by and promoted our offerings, which increased how many customers were flying in the door.

Then, just after noon, a customer called and said her sugar cookies tasted salty. Leon walked over to the table, picked up the sugar shaker, unscrewed the lid, and tasted the contents. Sure enough, someone had accidentally filled the sugar shaker with salt, and we had delivered hundreds of dozens of cookies coated with table salt instead of sugar. We scrambled to remake and redeliver, as more and more complaints came in, but the wheels were starting to come off.

Next, we started getting calls and emails from customers asking why their morning delivery was never made. We checked our system and couldn't find one ticket, then another, then another. We had no record of these orders. Our online orders came in via email, and we'd then key them into our proprietary software; the two systems weren't connected. All of a sudden, we knew what had happened: a huge number of orders that had come in over the past few weeks had been marked "read" but were never entered into the system. We didn't have a deposit or credit card reconciling process, which would have caught this problem early, so until that moment, we had no idea we had overlooked these orders.

We rushed to go back through our emails and find as many missed orders as we could, but the damage was done. Hundreds of orders hadn't been made. We'd already passed the delivery time for many of them, and squeezing in the others before the day ended was barely possible on top of the mess that was already going on in our chaotic kitchens. The rest of the day was spent trying to claw our way out and ended with us personally delivering to people late into the night and profusely apologizing for the fiasco.

Not delivering someone's Valentine's Day order is a big deal. They counted on us to make their loved one feel special, and we let them down in a major way. By midnight, we were exhausted and drained. We drove to Whataburger and in between ordering hamburgers and picking them up at the second window, we sat in the car and bawled. It was one of the worst Valentine's Days we'd ever had, and we had only ourselves to blame.

Even though the salt had nothing to do with the bigger problem of the missed orders, we coined the phrase "salt in the sugar shaker" because that was the moment everything started spiraling out of control. If we were sloppy and didn't make sure the sugar shakers were filled with sugar and not salt, we should expect that other things weren't being properly cared for either. Because of that failure, we knew we needed to make lots of changes, including tying the order taking and order processing systems together, reconciling deposits as a fail-safe, labeling the sugar and salt better, and tidying up all of our processes. We learned a valuable lesson: details matter, and if you don't get them right every day, it will end in disaster on the day it truly counts. When Leon walks into a store, he sprinkles a little sugar on his hand and tastes it, just to be sure it's sugar.

With each failure we experience, we continue to learn lessons—and we have no shortages of failures to learn from. What's most important is that afterward, we pick ourselves up and make sure we never do it again.

GET COMFORTABLE WITH HARD WORK

Leon

Although there's a lot of great advice out there, we continue to return to a foundational idea that's underrated, because there's no trick or hack for old-fashioned hard work. Here's what we tell ourselves and our team: There is so much about life and business that is out of your control. There will always be somebody who is smarter than you, who is better connected than you, who has more money than you, and who might be luckier than you. You can't control those things. The only thing you do have control over is how hard you work. One of my favorite quotes (which is attributed to athlete Jerry Rice) is, "Today I do what others won't, so tomorrow I can do what others can't."

PRIORITIZE EXECUTION OVER IDEAS

Tiff

People often mistakenly think that business success is based on one great idea or a series of great ideas. They say, "Warm-cookie delivery! I wish I had thought of that idea!" This always makes us smile because we wish it were that easy—to simply have a great idea and then everything else falls into place. While bright ideas are essential, execution is often overlooked.

Whenever we have management meetings at Tiff's Treats, I'm more interested in discussing how to better execute our current plans than in brainstorming new ideas. It's easy to brainstorm but much harder to bring it all to life. At one point during our growth, we were planning to hire our first PR agency. Since this was our first partnership of this kind, we didn't know what to expect. They sat us down and talked us through all kinds of ideas for promoting our newest store, which were sure to lead to success.

At the end of the hour-long pitch, I asked a basic question: "Who enacts all of these ideas?"

"Why, you do, of course!" they replied.

With mainly just the two of us as the corporate team, we had neither the time nor the resources to act on any of their ideas. We decided against hiring that firm. Coming up with ideas wasn't an issue—getting everything done was. That remains true today. If you have no way to execute a plan, there's no sense in dreaming it up.

BRING ON THE RIGHT PEOPLE

Leon

One ingredient that any successful business must have is the *right people* at the *right time*. Throughout our careers, we've been fortunate to work with smart, capable people. In the early days, we made things up as we went along and had a hardworking, driven team that did whatever it took to make ends meet and survive. Our tight-knit group in those early years arrived early, stayed late, and much more, all in the name of building the brand. Outsiders would look at us and wonder what in the world we were doing, but that didn't matter to us. We were all-in together as one team, striving to do what had never been done before in an industry that had never existed before. It took a group of special believers.

As we grew, we had to make room for new team members, who brought in best practices and more experience. In 2017, we started our search for a chief operating officer (COO) to help us build the infrastructure for rapid expansion. We were looking for someone who had experience in a similar industry and could infuse both professionalism and new ideas into our business. The search took over a year because Tiff and I knew exactly what we needed: someone with big-company experience who could think and act like an entrepreneur as well. This person also had to understand what we were trying to do and how important it was that we stay true to our brand and our Tiff's Top Five as we grew. And most importantly, this person had to believe in us and what we were doing.

The wait was worth it: Adam, who had held a leadership position at Domino's Pizza, became our COO. His joining our team meant a lot to us because, for the first time, somebody in a high-ranking position in a multibillion-dollar company was willing to risk their career by joining us.

Tiff

Adam brought a whole new perspective on how to best scale the business. While we'd been busy perfecting systems and centralizing control and decision-making, we'd inadvertently left our operations team without the empowerment or skills to solve their own problems. This became apparent one evening at closing time, when a manager on duty threw away an order that hadn't been picked up. The customer arrived five minutes late, only to find out their cookies had been tossed. When we asked why the manager had trashed the order rather than calling the customer to ask about their arrival time and letting them know the store was closing, the answer was simple: it wasn't on the closing instructions list.

We'd implemented so many rules and processes that we accidentally created leaders who were afraid to take any action that wasn't on a checklist, regardless of whether or not it made common sense. Under Adam's leadership, we learned that the only way to scale was to release control and allow store-level leaders to take ownership of their location's performance. This approach has made all the difference in the world in our ability to grow, and we owe a huge debt of gratitude to Adam for taking a leap of faith and joining us when he did.

Building and growing a business takes all different kinds of people and skill sets. To get where we are today, we needed all those fantastic people who joined early on every bit as much as we need Adam and the other professionals who have joined the team since. Though our business has needed different things at different times, the one constant requirement has been good people.

Leon

We have found our own recipe for success and feel that a lot of the lessons we've learned can be applied in many other situations. However, much like a family recipe that's passed down from generation to generation, each person should add their own ingredients and tweak each recipe to better suit his or her specific skills, talents, and situation. As anyone grows their business or tries to achieve career success, mistakes will happen. God knows Tiff and I have made many. One of the tenets we try to live by and preach in our organization is that it's okay to make one million mistakes—as long as you do your best to never make the same mistake twice.

Lemon Berry Trifle

The great thing about cookies is that they're versatile. Trifles usually use pound cake, but this recipe substitutes our Lemon Sugar Cookies, which adds a bright and flavorful element that is as pretty as it is delicious. Offset by the tart berries and smooth whipped topping, this light dessert is the perfect treat to "wow" at a party. It's quick to assemble but even quicker to devour. I challenge you to eat only one serving.

LEMON BERRY TRIFLE

PREP TIME: 60 MINUTES

BAKE TIME: 9 TO 11 MINUTES

MAKES 15 SERVINGS

LEMON SUGAR COOKIES

1 ⅛ cups (2 ¼ sticks) salted butter, softened

1 cup granulated white sugar

½ cup firmly packed light brown sugar

2 large eggs

1 teaspoon vanilla extract

1 ½ teaspoons salt

½ teaspoon baking soda

1 ¼ teaspoons lemon extract

2 ¼ cups all-purpose flour

FILLING

16 ounces fresh strawberries

4 ounces white chocolate baking bar (to make chocolate shavings)

2 (8-ounce) tubs whipped topping, defrosted overnight

12 ounces fresh raspberries

Preheat the oven to 375 degrees.

In a large mixing bowl, cream the butter, white sugar, and brown sugar together using a hand/electric mixer on medium speed until the mixture is smooth. Add the eggs, vanilla, salt, and baking soda to the butter mixture. Mix on medium speed until the ingredients are incorporated and smooth. Whisk in the lemon extract.

Add the flour. Mix on low speed until the flour is no longer loose, then on medium speed until the flour is fully incorporated.

Line a cookie sheet with parchment paper. Using a medium-sized cookie scooper, scoop the cookie dough (approximately 2 tablespoons each) onto the cookie sheet, placing the scoops at least 2 inches apart. Bake for 9 to 11 minutes, until the edges are browned and set.

Slide the parchment paper with cookies off the cookie sheet and directly onto the counter for cooling. (If not using parchment paper, let the cookies sit for 1 minute and then remove them to cool on the counter or a wire rack). Cool completely for 30 minutes.

Chop the strawberries into quarters.

Use a vegetable peeler to create white chocolate shavings by shaving down the length of the flat end of the white chocolate baking bar.

Cut the cooled cookies into quarters.

Layer half of the cookie quarters in the bottom of a 9-inch trifle dish (cookies can overlap). Spoon one 8-ounce container of defrosted whipped topping onto the cookie layer and spread evenly with the spoon.

Sprinkle half the chopped strawberries and half the raspberries onto the whipped topping layer.

Place the remaining half of the cookie quarters on top of the fruit layer. Spoon the other 8-ounce container of defrosted whipped topping onto the cookie layer and spread evenly with the spoon.

Sprinkle the remaining half of the strawberries and raspberries onto the whipped topping layer. Top with white chocolate shavings.

Serve immediately and refrigerate leftovers.

Molten Lava Cookies

Leon's favorite dessert at any restaurant is molten lava cake. That got me thinking about how we could turn that fun and rich treat into a cookie. These cookies have a melty ganache surprise center, and the flavor is out of this world. They take extra time, but the effort pays off. Easy yet impressive, these cookies are best served about fifteen minutes out of the oven, when they're sturdy enough to be picked up, but the chocolate is warm enough to run out of the center.

MOLTEN LAVA COOKIES

PREP TIME: 1 1/2 HOURS

BAKE TIME: 10 TO 12 MINUTES

MAKES 2 1/2 DOZEN COOKIES

GANACHE FILLING

1/2 cup heavy whipping
cream

3/4 cup semisweet
chocolate chips

CHOCOLATE COOKIES

1 1/8 cups (2 1/4 sticks)
salted butter, softened

1 cup granulated white
sugar

1/2 cup firmly packed light
brown sugar

2 large eggs

2 teaspoons vanilla extract

1 1/2 teaspoons salt

1/2 teaspoon baking soda

2 2/3 cups all-purpose flour

1/2 cup cocoa

1/4 cup powdered sugar

In a small pot, heat the heavy cream to a simmer. Do not bring it to a boil.

Add the chocolate chips to a small bowl and pour the warm cream over the chocolate. Slowly stir until the chocolate is melted and the mixture is smooth. Refrigerate the ganache mixture for one hour, until firm.

In a large mixing bowl, cream the butter, white sugar, and brown sugar together using a hand/electric mixer on medium speed until the mixture is smooth.

Add the eggs, vanilla, salt, and baking soda to the butter mixture. Mix on medium speed until the ingredients are incorporated and smooth.

Add the flour and cocoa. Mix on low speed until the flour is no longer loose, then on medium speed until the flour is fully incorporated.

Preheat the oven to 375 degrees, then refrigerate the cookie dough for 30 minutes.

Line a cookie sheet with parchment paper. Using a teaspoon, scoop the cooled ganache into balls and place them onto the cookie sheet. Place the sheet in the freezer for 30 minutes.

Scoop the cookie dough using a medium-sized cookie scooper packed flat (not rounded). Use the palm of your hand to flatten the cookie scoop into a pancake.

Place one frozen ganache ball into the center of the flat dough and wrap the dough around it. Roll the dough in your palms to make a firm, smooth ball of dough, making sure to keep the ganache fully inside.

Line another cookie sheet with parchment paper. Place the dough balls on the cookie sheet, at least 2 inches apart. Bake for 10 to 12 minutes.

Slide the parchment paper with cookies off the cookie sheet and directly onto the counter for cooling. (If not using parchment paper, let sit on the tray for cooling.)

Allow the cookies to cool slightly, about 15 minutes, before handling. You will not be able to pick up the hot cookies without them falling apart. Sprinkle powdered sugar on top of the finished cookies.

Serve immediately. When torn open, the chocolate center of the cookie will spill out like molten lava cake.

Note: Molten Lava Cookies have a shelf life of 2 days at room temperature.

Warm Moment

I hope this reaches somebody high up in the business.

I want to thank you for existing. For being such a bringer of joy and an accessible outlet for friends and family to surprise one another with the comfort of a warm cookie. Such a wonderful concept. And you've maintained excellence for the years I've been a customer. Thank you.

My wife and I just experienced a miscarriage. And the outpouring of love and support from our family and friends has been amazing. One way they've cheered us up: your cookies. We've had three deliveries in two days. A few of those orders were made online by out-of-town family. And they accomplish their mission. Biting into a warm cookie and washing it down with some cold milk—does it get any better? A moment of escape from our grief and a reminder that we are loved and have so much to be grateful for.

Thank you. You help people celebrate; you help them grieve; you help them say "I love you"; you help them say "happy birthday"; you help them say "thinking about you." You help people. You truly make a difference. And we've noticed.

—Eric and Jodi

CONCLUSION

We are so grateful for the journey we've been on the past twenty-plus years. As some of the stories we've shared throughout this book have shown, we've failed hilariously and unequivocally and had some stressful times. We gave a lot to build this brand but have received a hundred times more in the form of unique experiences, fun memories, and lifelong friendships. And some of our favorite moments will be from the days we could barely make rent or payroll.

We never could have imagined that a missed date and a batch of cookies would lead to such a rich and fulfilled life for us, both personally and professionally. We are proof that the American dream exists. Every day we get to work with people we admire and love, while providing the world with happiness. And the two of us get to do it together.

As you're growing a business, it's easy to become wrapped up in the company's financial metrics. College-aged Tiff and Leon had no idea they'd build a business that one day would raise over $100 million from investors and be worth many times that amount. While that's important to the business, it's merely the byproduct of our true purpose: connecting people through warm moments. We're able to make that human connection in a world that's more divided and isolated than ever before.

When we started out, we had little vision for what this company would become. We thought we were building a cookie company, and serving convenient sweet treats was our only mission. Over time, we realized how much we underestimated the role we'd be honored to play in helping people celebrate all of life's moments. It's easy to see now that it's not, and never was, just about the cookies.

—TIFF AND LEON

ACKNOWLEDGMENTS

Special thanks go out to Carolyn, Deepti, and the whole testing squad at Tiff's Treats, for the late-night cookie baking and recipe tweaking. To Leslie and Sam, for arriving just in time to coordinate all the book efforts. To our publishing partners, for your trust and encouragement, and for bringing this book to life. To our family and friends, who mean everything to us. To the entire Tiff's Treats family, past and present, for helping us deliver warm moments across the country, and for building something special together. And finally, thanks to our customers and fans, whose support has kept us going through all the ups and downs, and who have invited us to be a part of special moments in their lives. We are humbled by and grateful for you all.

ABOUT THE AUTHORS

Tiffany Chen, president of Tiff's Treats, graduated with a bachelor of science in advertising from the University of Texas. In 1999, she cofounded the nation's first warm-cookie delivery company with her then-boyfriend, now-husband Leon Chen. She has spent the past twenty years growing Tiff's Treats as cofounder and president, and the past seven years as mom to the couple's twins.

Leon Chen is the cofounder, chairman, and CEO of Tiff's Treats. Leon has served on several nonprofit boards, including Foster Angels of Central Texas, The Fifty, and the Greater Austin Chamber of Commerce. He is a mentor with SKU, an Austin-based consumer packaged goods incubator, and he sat on the board of directors for Epic, which was acquired by General Mills in 2016.